Katie Piper is a presenter and charity campaigner. In 2008 she survived a rape and acid attack that left her facially disfigured. Her moving, BAFTA-nominated Channel 4 documentary *Katie: My Beautiful Face* was watched by 3.5 million viewers and shown in more than 15 countries, including ABC in America. Katie founded her own charity to help people living with burns and scars and recently received a prestigious Woman of the Year award.

'Some people have a special aura about them. They exude a certain kind of confidence and calm that makes everyone around them feel better. Katie Piper is one of those people . . . [*Beautiful Ever After*] is a testimony to the strength of the human spirit' *Best*

'Katie Piper is an extraordinary woman . . . It is impossible not to be moved by the events described' *Mail on Sunday*

'A touching read' *New!*

'An emotional rollercoaster' *Star*

Katie Piper

Beautiful Ever After

Quercus

For my Big Pug

First published in Great Britain in hardback in 2014 by
Quercus Editions Ltd

This paperback edition published in 2015 by
Quercus Editions Ltd
55 Baker Street
7th Floor, South Block
London
W1U 8EW

PICTURE CREDITS
SECTION 1
p1 Daily Mirror Pride of Britain Awards/Pete Mariner;
p2 top Daily Mirror Pride of Britain Awards; bottom Mirrorpix/Phil Harris;
p3 Rex/Jonathan Hordle

SECTION 2
p1 Fabulous/© David Bailey; p3 Rex/Roger Askew;
p4 Rex/Jonathan Hordle; p6 Getty/Neil P Mockford

All other pictures supplied by the author.

A CIP catalogue record for this book is available
from the British Library.

PB ISBN 978 1 78429 116 7
Ebook ISBN 978 1 78087 657 3

10 9 8 7 6 5 4 3 2 1

Consultant: Clare O'Reilly

Text designed and typeset by IDSUK (Data Connection) Ltd
Printed and bound in Great Britain by Clays Ltd, St Ives plc

July 2013

To my baby,

Right now you're growing safe and warm in my tummy, your whole life stretching out ahead of you. Your possibilities are endless. You're perfect. You can be whoever you want to be, do whatever you want to do, go wherever you want to go. Your potential is limitless. I wanted to write you this letter so you can always look back and know how much you have been loved, right from the minute we first knew you were coming into our lives.

Though I'm your mum, you will be in charge of your own destiny. I can try and steer you, try and advise you, but if you're anything like I was as a child, you'll always make your own choices and forge your own path, learning as much from your failures as from your successes.

I've thought long and hard about what I want for you in your lifetime. It'd be simple for me to say I'd love you to be a doctor like Mr Jawad, the man who saved my life and gave me back my face, but there are also far simpler things I want for you; basic building blocks which will make you happy, foundations that have nothing to do with your career path or future decisions.

I want you to be healthy and never to know physical pain, the smell of hospitals or the bleeps of machines. I want you to be strong, both physically and mentally. You will always be able to lean on your dad and me, but finding your own strength inside and knowing you can rely on it will carry you through whatever hardships life throws at you.

I want you to be fearless and free and confident. Don't live by anyone else's rules; I hope you design and live by your own. Don't measure yourself against others; fulfil your own potential. As long as you can look at yourself in the mirror and swear with unflinching honesty that you're the best version of yourself you can be, you'll always sleep well and feel proud of who you are.

I want you to be tender and gentle, but fierce and brave. I want you to see the best in everything, the light in the dark, the hope in despair. I want you to know compassion and never to judge. Everyone has their own story; you never know what's going on inside them.

I will always try to protect you from evil but I will also teach you that there are a vast many more good people in the world than there are bad. I'll help you understand that life can be hard sometimes and can rip you from the path you thought you were on, but with strength and courage you can grow to accept and love the new path you have to carve out for yourself, and you can reach the destination that was meant for you nonetheless.

You will grow up seeing disfigurement as a badge of honour, not one of shame. A mark of how far people have come, not of how different they are. You, my miracle child, will learn that beauty is only skin deep and that the courage in your heart will carry you further in life than the shape of your cheek bones. This is everything I now know to be true and hold dear.

I want us to be close always. I want to make you proud of me and I want you to know I'm always here, that there's nothing I won't do for you, and that my love for you is infinite. I hope you won't take it for granted, but don't ever doubt its existence.

We'll find our way on this journey together; we will learn, explore and grow together. After all, we're both new to this, and while I'm filled with fear and trepidation about getting it right and not messing up, my heart is bursting with love for you, and that feels like a pretty good starting place.

Love,

Mummy x

Chapter One

As the faint blue line grew stronger, so did my heart, beating in my chest. Pregnant. Pregnant with the impossible. Pregnant with my future. Pregnant with my happily ever after. Pregnant with the child I'd believed to my core would never grow inside me.

But soon elation and shock gave way to a deep feeling of unease and fear about a future so precious. The weight of responsibility felt overwhelming. How would I keep my child safe? Away from hurt and harm? How could I look my child in the eye and promise my protection? Promise that I'd keep him or her safe from evil when I know what brutality exists in this world?

I was just twenty-four years old when, in 2008, my ex-boyfriend Danny Lynch got a man named Stefan Sylvestre to throw industrial-strength sulphuric acid in my face, burning away the old Katie Piper and changing my life forever. Three days before, Danny had raped me, beaten me and held me hostage in a hotel room for hours. After finally letting me go, he'd convinced me not to go to the police. I'd then avoided him completely until he sent me a series of begging texts, pleading with me to go to an internet cafe to read an email he said he'd sent me. I stepped out from my

London flat into the cold March air, already a shadow of the care-free, twenty-something Katie I'd been just days earlier. When the large cupful of acid hit my smooth, soft, line-free skin, trickling down my throat and partially blinding me, he almost succeeded in extinguishing the last of the old Katie. Almost.

As I felt the searing heat and smelled my burning flesh, I was sure I was going to die. I didn't, but I have spent the six years since going in and out of hospital, enduring over 250 operations and working through thousands of hours of counselling and therapy to help me cope with both the emotional and physical scars that the attack left me with.

For the longest time I was certain that my chances of a normal future had gone. In the immediate aftermath of the attack I was horrified by my own reflection, barely recognising the image of myself in the mirror. I would play back memories of all the relationships I'd ever had, trying to ingrain images and emotions into my mind of what it felt like to be loved, to hold hands, to kiss. I was sure that if I survived I'd never be attractive to anyone again, never be intimate, never be wanted. Never be loved.

Then in 2011, when I was told that the drugs I'd been prescribed to help restore my vision could have a huge effect on my fertility, I spent months reconciling myself to the idea that, even if I did find love, I'd probably never bear my own child. I would never experience a swollen belly and feel butterfly kicks in my tummy. Little did I know what my future held, and how I would be proved wrong on this too.

So, in July 2013, when I finally saw the positive pregnancy test – my blue lifeline from the future – it presented me with endless possibilities and infinite opportunities, but it also gripped me in a tailspin of fear.

I wondered: would a daughter be able to relate to me, a disfigured woman who just happened to be her mum? I instantly started trying to formulate an explanation that would be suitable for little ears about why Mummy looks the way she does. Tried to figure out how to explain that I used to look like everyone else. How would I tell my child what had happened to me without it sounding terrifying? How would we both cope with being stared at on the school run and how would it feel to have little hands run over my scars, which only my loved ones have touched in tenderness?

Among all the normal worries about whether I'd be a good mother, I also found myself thinking, what if I have a girl? What if my daughter has my old face? The one I lost at the age of twenty-four. How would it feel to see my face staring back at me, and to know what I would have looked like at thirty, forty, even fifty? I'd be able to see how my wrinkles might have set in. Where my laughter lines would have been. The answers to all of these questions would be reflected back at me in one exquisite face that I'd helped create.

It felt like an uneasy admission, but I thought I'd worry less about a son than a daughter. A boy wouldn't need as much protection as a girl would. A son could be strong enough to fight someone off, prevent an attack, run to safety. A son might be safe walking down a dark alley at night. A son might not be attacked, have acid thrown in his face . . . But a daughter might. As I wrapped my arms around my stomach, I felt a surge of protectiveness I'd never known before. I had to keep my child safe. I *had* to. But how would I protect my dream-come-true when I hadn't been able to protect myself on that cold spring day in 2008?

My trembling began to subside and the faint blue lines grew stronger, along with my resolve. I'd defied the odds before and I'd do it again. I wasn't supposed to survive having my face burned off with acid, I was supposed to crawl into a hole and disappear, or even die, but I'd refused. I'd feared I was infertile but I wasn't. Feared I was too scarred to find my happily ever after, and yet I'd found love. I was about to become a mother and bring a child into this world, and start a future filled with love, happiness and positivity. A future I'd never have dared to dream of when I moved out of my parents' house and into my own home, alone, three years earlier.

* * *

In the early spring of 2010, after two years of hard recovery, I finally felt strong enough to contemplate living an independent life and to move out of my parents' house in Hampshire, having been cared for and looked after by them for so long. I had no idea what the future held for me, or how I would cope without them by my side on a daily basis, but there was no way of finding out unless I made the leap.

Since the attack I had needed my parents to hold my hand, assuage my fears, dry my tears, and help me medically, physically and mentally. But as my body had grown stronger, I slowly began to crave the freedom and independence I'd had before the attack. I longed to have my life back and be in control of it again, and not to have to depend on anyone for anything. I was petrified, but also excited; I was sure it was the right thing to do, the start of the next chapter in my life, and that it would help move me further along the road to being 'normal' again.

At first I started flat-hunting in secret, fearing my parents would try to persuade me to stay at home under their watchful eye. They were desperately worried about me, but despite their concerns I knew I was ready to push myself forward.

I began looking around West London to be near my work at the Katie Piper Foundation, which I'd set up the year before and had been commuting to daily from Hampshire. At first I tried to find a place in a concierge building with underground parking and security gates; the things I thought I'd need in order to feel safe, but it quickly became apparent they weren't the things a girl in her mid-twenties could afford. I soon had to make compromises, challenging as that was to my courage. Bit by bit, the 'must haves' on my list got crossed off and by late spring I had narrowed down my options to a shortlist of three flats.

I plucked up the courage to share my plan with Mum and Dad, explaining all my thinking and rationale, hoping they'd see that I hadn't rushed into any decision-making. As predicted they were, understandably, anxious, but they knew that me pushing myself out of my comfort zone was an important next step for me, and that I was as determined about this as I have been about all stages of my recovery. So, once they realised they couldn't dissuade me, they gave me their usual incredible support, which gave me even more strength. I think they were delighted that I'd come so far, they'd thought it would be years yet until I was ready to live on my own. They were a bit surprised I'd been looking at places without their knowledge, but I could tell by their shared glances they were also secretly proud of me too. The defiant Kate was back again and it was a glimpse of the independent daughter that they had raised but had missed so sorely for the last two years.

I talked them through my shortlist of flats and with their wisdom of experience they helped me weigh up the pros and cons of each until I made my final choice: a cute little one-bedroom flat in Chiswick. It was tiny but it was set on a quiet road and it felt secure enough for me. The fact that it was on the first floor made me feel a bit less exposed – ground-floor and basement flats carry a higher risk of burglary. My staircase helped me feel more comfortable that I was further away from possible danger.

As an added bonus, there was a police detective living downstairs; I'd met him while the sale was going through when Dad and I had gone over to do some measuring. He was familiar with my story and I overheard him tell Dad he'd do his best to keep an eye on me, which was reassuring for both me and Dad. Having one of the Met's finest living below me was the next best thing to secure parking and a concierge.

My parents were incredible in the lead-up to moving day. They helped me pack up all my things and a fair few of theirs! I'd stretched myself financially to buy the flat, which meant I couldn't yet afford to furnish it properly (which I was determined to do so myself), so Mum came to the rescue, begging and borrowing as much second-hand cutlery and crockery as she could from family and friends. She and Dad lent me their old garden furniture to use in the lounge, and offered a camp bed as a short-term solution until I could buy a proper one.

Then the big day finally arrived to leave my old home and old life and start my new life in my new home. My parents were tireless helpers, and we loaded up my VW Beetle and their car until they were both bursting at the seams. I gave our dog Barclay a huge hug goodbye, telling him I'd be back soon to visit, and we set off for Chiswick. I felt a twinge of emotion as I drove away, knowing it would be as big a transition for my parents as it was for me. I knew we'd miss one another's constant company, and that this day was highly symbolic of our triumph as a family over what had happened to me. I was, and am, so grateful to my parents, as much for allowing me the room to grow and be free as for helping put me back together again when I was too weak to help myself.

We arrived at my flat and spent many hours shifting all my things up the stairs of my building and then unpacking all the boxes and bags. At the end of moving day my flat looked like a squat with all the temporary furniture, empty boxes and the explosion of stuff. But none of it mattered – I was just so proud to be in this new place, both literally and metaphorically.

When everything was set up, we went out to get something to eat and over dinner Mum and Dad gently questioned whether I wanted company on my first night. Mum spoke first.

'Kate, love, are you sure you don't want us to stay with you tonight?'

None of us voiced it at the time but I know now that we were all as nervous as one another.

'Mum, I'm fine, honestly. I'm just going to have a cuppa, read for a while and go to bed.'

I could tell by the look on her face she didn't completely believe me.

'Promise you'll call us tonight before you turn in?'

'I promise, Mum, and thanks for helping today.'

When they left later that evening, I watched them drive away and wanted to show them I was tough, so I smiled and waved until they were out of view. I'd already given them enough sleepless nights, and I wanted them to rest easy knowing I was happy, confident and strong in my decision, even though I was secretly trembling inside with the unknown before me.

Just two hours later I was faced with my first big test when the power went off, sending me into darkness without warning. I felt searing fear surge through me, and I was sure that this was my attackers returning, coming to finish me off. I spoke out loud to try to talk myself through it.

'Calm down, Kate. Deep breaths. Take a look out of the window and see if anyone else has lost power too.'

Sure enough, the entire street had been plunged into darkness. I let out a sigh of relief. After feeling my way to the kitchen to find the torch that Mum had insisted I take from home, I knew I needed to hear her and Dad's voices, so I found my phone and called to tell them what had happened as the torch flickered and spluttered. Dad was adamant I come home straight away.

'Kate, I can come and get you if you'd rather not drive. Don't sit there in the dark all night, you've no idea when the power will go back on.'

His offer was tempting: this was a pretty odd first night! A huge part of me wanted to take him up on it, but I resolved to stay put. Knowing I had a police officer living downstairs gave me the extra bit of courage I needed.

'Dad, I'm okay, honestly. It's only a power cut, and I have the torch. I'm about to go to bed anyway and I don't need lights while I'm asleep, so I'll be fine. I just wanted to let you know what was going on. That's all.'

He made me promise to call if I changed my mind, whatever time of night it might be. It made me feel stronger having them there if I needed them. After hanging up, I crawled under the duvet on my camp bed and read a magazine in the dwindling torchlight until I fell asleep.

I woke the next morning to find the power had come back on. Mum and Dad called first thing to check I'd survived the night. I had, and it was my first triumph living on my own.

Chapter Two

I began settling into a regular daily routine, which I hadn't dared dream I'd ever experience again. I might not have *looked* like every other girl in her late twenties, but with a job and a pokey little place to myself, eating microwave meals and running out of milk, I finally *felt* like lots of other girls my age again.

My medical treatment was (and continues to be) ongoing, but the masks I'd had to wear for twenty-three hours a day to help compress my scars were a distant memory, packed away in a box in Mum and Dad's garage. The Foundation wasn't even a year old yet but we were receiving hundreds of emails every week in response to my documentary, *Katie: My Beautiful Face*, which had been shown on Channel 4 in October 2009.

It was a huge boost to my confidence when kind strangers approached me to say they'd seen the documentary and how much they'd been moved by it. Many were keen to tell me about the personal challenges they too had overcome. To this day, it never fails to amaze and touch me when people open up to me. It always makes me feel like I'm part of a special group of survivors, a secret society of people who 'made it', people who've been tested to their limits but have come back fighting, who have rebuilt themselves – emotionally, physically or both. These people make me feel like anything is possible. Though what happened to me may be written all over my face, I know hundreds – thousands – of survivors who've fought hard to recover from trauma, attacks or abuse, and yet you'd never know it to look at them. They wear their scars on the inside, but those scars are just as real as ones on the outside. Being part of that group – having unflinching and unwavering support from people I hardly know – will always make me feel like anything is possible.

And it was these feelings and a desire to help this amazing group of survivors that had made me set up the Foundation in the first place. And now the charity was keeping me busier than I could ever have imagined and my diary was filling up weeks in advance. I loved how fast the Foundation was growing but I felt a huge responsibility to make sure we stayed on top of everything. I'd work long and late into the night, making sure I'd replied to everyone who'd contacted us. Dinners for one from Sainsbury's were replaced with snacks from the office vending machines. I'd sneak down the hall, trying not to get noticed by people from the other businesses on our floor who were also working late, but my clacking heels always blew my cover and inevitably I'd be spotted sneaking back with my two-course dinner of Mini Cheddars and Maltesers. Setting out my feast in front of my computer screen I felt secure and safe, cocooned in a job I loved. If you had told me years earlier that I'd be running a charity, I'd never have believed you; never have thought I was capable of opening a spreadsheet, let alone writing financial plans and building a charity.

In addition to the growing commitments at the Foundation, I was getting more and more requests for interviews and offers of television work as well as writing my own columns. It was a huge confidence boost, but I could only be in so many places at once, and there was so much I didn't know how to negotiate. It soon became obvious that I needed an agent to help guide me.

I turned to Mags, the PR lady at Channel 4 who'd worked on my documentary, and she introduced me to a great agent, Joanne. We bonded straight away and she instantly made life easier; it was a huge relief having her manage my diary and help me navigate the alien media world. And being freed from answering all the daily requests gave me much more time to concentrate on developing the Foundation.

My career was really taking off now, so I felt it was time to focus a bit more on the longer term and where I'd be in six months or a year. It was scary at first thinking that far ahead, as it wasn't something I'd done much of since the attack. For so long I'd just focused on getting through the hour or day or week. But allowing myself to dream and think ahead helped to put the past behind me.

In June 2010, I got some mind-blowing news: my documentary was nominated for a BAFTA. The film had been gruelling to make, not only because it meant reliving the horrors of what happened to me and revealing some of my most private, painful experiences to an unknown audience, but it also meant documenting the sentencing of the men who had attacked me and my reaction to it – I had no idea at the time what the outcome was going to be. So, in addition to the overwhelming public support I received when the film aired, getting the BAFTA nomination went some way to confirming that I had made the right decision to share my story. While we didn't win at the actual awards ceremony, it was still one of the most memorable nights of my life and the whole experience was elating.

A few weeks later, still on a high from the BAFTAs, I was in a meeting with Joanne to talk about new projects when she announced she had a surprise for me. Victoria Beckham's agent had sent me some perfume, body lotion, sunglasses and Victoria's style book in a beautifully wrapped box. Tucked inside was a handwritten note from Posh herself, telling me she thought I was brave and inspiring and should stay fabulous always. I nearly fainted. I looked at Joanne in total astonishment, and blurted out, 'The Victoria Beckham? Writing to ME??' I pulled myself together and wrote a note straight back to thank her for being so incredibly thoughtful.

The minute I left Joanne's office I was straight on the phone to my sister, Suzy. I couldn't dial fast enough! I was so excited to tell her what had just happened; she knew how much I loved the Spice Girls. We used to dress up and sing *Wannabe* with our cousin (I was Baby because of my blonde hair), and now I had a letter and gifts from Posh! If that wasn't enough, shortly afterwards Victoria's agent got in touch again and said that if I ever wanted to borrow a dress for an event I should just let her know. It was like being invited to play in her closet – the best closet in the whole world, belonging to one of my idols. It was a girl's dream come true.

I hoped that some day I'd be able to take her up on it, but right then I had plenty to keep me busy at the Foundation and a glamorous night out seemed a world away. Staying on top of my daily admin and responding to everyone who wrote in to us, thanking strangers for donations, or making sure we sent out fundraising tins, t-shirts and kits for people who wanted to hold events to raise money for us was practically a full-time job, even with a growing staff of three. But I was also about to embark upon a huge new project that was going to take things to a whole new level.

In the weeks following the BAFTAs, Joanne was handling even more media requests and we were on and off the phone several times a day. Despite all the attention, I've never seen myself as a celebrity. I was and always will be just Katie Piper. I still travel on the Tube, join the queue, take the rubbish out and clean the house. I see myself as a woman who had a high-profile news story attached to her, which now brings me a lot of warmth and love, both in person and in the virtual world through online messages or tweets.

But soon I got a call that knocked me sideways with disbelief – a publisher had been in touch with Joanne and wanted me to write my story. I had never even considered that I might write a book one day, let alone that anyone would want to read it, so it was a huge surprise when they expressed interest. Joanne told me she'd handle everything regarding the details and the contract, but in order to make the most of all the publicity I was getting at the time the publisher had set a deadline of just a few short months. All I had to do was to get writing – fast! While it felt daunting and like totally unfamiliar territory, I was really excited – I'm always up for a challenge!

We met with the publisher and the team, talked everything through about how I would tell my story, and set the publication date for the start of 2011. We even settled on a title: *Beautiful*. I had first reclaimed the word in the title of my documentary; it's a word that resonates with women across the globe, but it means something very different to me. I may have been beautiful before the attack, but while I recovered I learned the true meaning of inner beauty, both in myself and in others, and I wanted to open more people's eyes and hearts to the meaning of true beauty.

I went home straight after the meeting and started to outline everything. I thought about how I could tell my story in more detail than I had been able to do in the documentary. I started the process of going through all my old journals, and reread all my thoughts and feelings about what had happened to me. It was so strange; it felt simultaneously distant, as if I were reading someone else's words, and like the feelings were completely fresh and had all happened just yesterday. The words in my diaries were so raw and honest; sometimes my directness surprised even me.

As with making the documentary, the process wasn't easy; in the years since the attack I had tried to push a lot of terrifying memories out of my head. As I wrote and rewrote, I had to work through the material several times, which meant I was going over and over these memories. Years before, when the trial for my attackers was finished, I'd put the judges' sentencing remarks away in a drawer and I hadn't read them since the end of the trial. I decided to read them again and choose which bits should be in the book. The judge had said, '[the victim] had a face of pure beauty. You, Danny Lynch and Stefan Sylvestre, represent the face of pure evil. . . . Her psychological injuries are severe. There is a significant risk of clinical depression with a degree of change of personality and self-harm. However, her tremendous courage is not in doubt . . . Her desire for justice and her unwavering truth-fulness in the face of the most appalling adversity were the clearest examples of the bravery of the human spirit.' Reading the words took me straight back to that day, and I remembered how I'd hoped Danny and Stefan's incarceration would be a magic wand to shut out everything that had happened to me, but in fact it had left me more rudderless than I'd ever imagined.

I wanted the book to include pictures to help show what my life was like both before and after the attack. I spent hours digging out old photos, searching for images of my old face and setting them next to pictures of me with my new face – my burned face, my scarred face, my masked face. It was something I hadn't really let myself do up until then; I had worked so hard to accept my new face in order to rebuild my life, stay positive and keep moving forward. So having the different Katies staring back at me from the pictures was a pretty big moment.

Writing *Beautiful* was a journey that took me to places I couldn't have predicted. Sometimes it was empowering to think how far I'd come in my healing, and at other times it was horrific and impos-sibly difficult to think back to what had happened to me. But ulti-mately it was a really cathartic experience getting it all out, and I was intensely proud of the result – not least because of the speed with which I'd had to write it.

All during this time I was also working on the filming of my second documentary for Channel 4, *Katie: My Beautiful Friends*, which was focusing on my setting up the charity and meeting other disfigured people who were trying to make their way in a world that is still often uneasy about disfigurement. One was a young woman named Adele, a teenage ballerina who had been scalded in the shower during an epileptic seizure and who was suffering from crushingly low self-esteem as a result of her injuries. Another was Amit, a man with neurofibromatosis, a disorder he'd had since birth in which nerve tissue grows into tumours. He was warm and funny, and was trying to make a happy life for himself in a world that isn't always willing to accept and embrace the way he looks.

Some, like Amit, had been living with disfigurement for far longer than I had, and each of us was at a different point in our recovery. But knowing the ambition of this programme was to educate the public about differences gave each and every one of us a sense of purpose and pride. I knew when the programme aired it would show the viewing public that people are far more similar than they are different, no matter how they look. After all, on the inside, we all want and deserve love, success, happiness and recognition.

The show was also documenting the Foundation's belated official launch, so we were working hard to make sure that when the show aired we had enough resources to cope with the swell of letters and emails we expected to receive.

But despite having so much going on in my life, after less than a year of living alone, the novelty of having a place to myself began to wear off and a loneliness I'd never expected started to seep in. The privacy I thought I'd cherish began to feel suffocating. When I'd lived away from Mum and Dad before the attack, I'd been in a shared house with lots of people coming and going, or organising nights out. But now, the TV was my only companion when nobody was around, and it became strangely important. I finally had a sofa, and I would curl up and watch a movie in comfort and try to distract myself from how lonely I was.

I soon grew bored of flicking between the few Freeview channels I liked, so, with my 'my house is my home' mantra in my head, I decided I'd treat myself to Sky TV.

But I faced an unexpected challenge when I phoned up Sky to get it connected – I was told an engineer would need to come out to install the box and dish.

'What, to my house?' I asked the advisor on the phone. I had presumed they just flipped a switch somewhere.

'Yes.'

'Where I live? Here?'

'Yes, we have to connect the box to your TV.'

My stomach flipped with anxiety. So far, only family and friends had set foot in my flat, and the thought of having a stranger in my home, a man I didn't know, filled me with dread. He'd know where I live, he'd have my address. I'd be alone with him. He could attack me, hurt me, do whatever he wanted and I'd be powerless to stop him.

I told the person on the phone that I needed to have a think and would call them back. I had to give myself a pep talk for a whole week before I felt strong enough to call again and make the appointment. I was terrified but I kept telling myself it'd be worth it when I could snuggle down with a tub of ice cream and *Sex And The City 2* after a long, hard week.

The day of the installation arrived. Shaking out my hands and taking deep breaths, I repeated a mantra over and over in my head: 'He's not going to hurt you; he's here to install Sky. There's nothing to be afraid of. Just focus on all the films you'll get to see . . .'

The doorbell rang, and I opened the door.

'Hi, I'm Pete from Sky, you're after a new box and a dish?'

I smiled nervously and let him in, retreating back to the front door as soon as I could. At least if he lunged at me I'd be able to get away. I noticed him looking at me curiously.

'Were you burned in a fire, love?'

I was so shocked that I barely knew what to say.

'Sorry?'

'Your face. Was it a house fire?'

He'd caught me completely off guard. Of all the scenarios I'd played out in my head, having a chat about my burned face wasn't one of them. I'd feared he was going to attack me, not make small talk. I touched my cheek and flipped my fringe lower down over my eyes.

'Yes. Yep. A house fire . . .'

The inner Katie started screaming. 'What are you doing? Why the hell did you tell him it was a house fire? Have you lost your mind? What if he recognises you? What if it was a test to see if you were telling the truth? You sound like an idiot.'

But I felt like I was on improvisation auto-pilot and couldn't stop myself.

'You poor love. I'm so sorry.'

Internal Katie hadn't finished with me yet. 'You are mental. Mental. What are you, some kind of lunatic? Just stop talking.'

Luckily, he decided not to probe further and steered the conversation on to the box before putting a dish on the wall outside and finally leaving.

Shutting the door, I collapsed onto the sofa and called my best friend Kay to tell her what an idiot I'd been. We had first met in the toilets of QVC while auditioning for a presenting job in our early twenties and she'd been a constant in my life ever since. Hearing her laughter made me see the funny side too.

The irony was that, after all the worry and stress about making the appointment, a few days later I received a formal letter from the Residents' Association of my building reminding me that we were in a conservation area, and as I hadn't got permission to put up a Sky dish, I'd have to take it down.

So with the dish gathering dust in a cupboard, and not much on TV to warrant staying in all the time, my weekend nights out started to extend to weeknights too, as much as my schedule would allow. Dinner with friends, nights down the pub, girly sleepovers, cinema trips and visits back home to Mum and Dad filled my evenings. I loved hanging out with friends, but before long it started to feel less like relaxed fun and more like a desperate attempt to spend as much time as possible away from the silence of my flat.

My weekdays were similar: I was packing in as much as I could, and pushing myself harder and harder at the Foundation, which aims to support people with burns and scars from trauma injuries and to improve scar management and burns rehabilitation in the UK.

I was working with hair restoration, permanent make-up and camouflage make-up specialists and I also ran workshops for people with burns and scars, to help build their confidence and to give them a chance to meet others and share experiences.

But still, the feelings of loneliness were growing even more acute, especially when I hung out with friends who were all loved-up. Kay had her fiancé, Ivan, and my school friend Juliet was moving in with her boyfriend, Mark. I watched them and other friends share their lives with their other halves. They had someone to eat with, laugh with, sleep with; someone to help them celebrate life's triumphs, and deal with the lows. I was genuinely happy for them but naturally I started longing for a relationship of my own, for someone to love. I had a career, great friends and a place of my own. A boyfriend seemed like the missing piece of the puzzle.

It wasn't that I hadn't had any relationships after the attack – I'd had a boyfriend when I still lived at home with my parents, but we'd split up just before I moved out. While he hadn't been my Mr Right, he'd certainly been my Mr Really Bloody Helpful. He'd given me confidence and helped me establish intimacy again, and because of him I felt there was hope for me to find someone who'd see past my scars and want the real me, and I was more than ready for that to happen.

Chapter Three

One Friday night, towards the end of 2010, I met up with Kay in a pub in Chiswick. I decided to share what I had been feeling.

'I think I'm ready to start dating again. . . What do you think?'

She looked at me as only a best friend can. 'Are you sure?'

She was sweetly protective of me.

'I think so,' I said, 'I know it probably won't happen straight away but inside I'm starting to feel like I did before the attack, more normal. I know I don't look the same, but frankly I want a boyfriend. I know I've got you and my other mates, but I'm tired of being lonely. Do you think anyone will want me?'

I felt desperately vulnerable as I asked the question. I knew Kay loved me but I also knew she'd be honest with me.

'Yes, Katie, I do. I really truly do.'

Over the next few months, I did start meeting a few guys, usually through friends on a night down the pub. But I soon noticed something odd happening. Often I'd get chatting to a guy and he would seem really interested in everything I said, and we'd end up talking all night. I'd get excited, feeling sure that he liked me, that we'd really connected. He'd ask for my number and I'd go home feeling great – sometimes daydreaming about the possibility of things progressing further. Then the next day I'd be gutted when a text message arrived, asking me to do something like open his village fete or draw the winning raffle ticket at his work Christmas do. It felt like these guys only wanted the public Katie, the one they'd seen on TV, not Katie the woman, who was awkwardly trying to find herself a boyfriend.

With others, I'd think I could sense a spark but after a few minutes' chat he'd be pouring his heart out to me, telling me such sad stories about the worst things that had happened to him, opening up to me as if I were a therapist. I wondered if these men thought I was out of bounds because of what I'd been through. That having been raped and left disfigured had made it impossible for me to fancy anyone or be fancied. It felt like I'd become asexual to men. Guys would approach me to tell me I was inspiring and amazing, which at the time was flattering and gave me hope and confidence, but then I'd watch them walk up to a girl who looked like I used to and ask for her phone number, and my heart would sink.

Sometimes they would even say things to me like, 'Bless you. You're so sweet and brave.' I'd smile outwardly, but inside I was so frustrated, thinking 'Oh my God, I'm nearly 27, what do you mean I'm so *sweet*?' I longed to be desirable, not sweet.

After many situations like these, I began to get a gnawing feeling inside that no one wanted me, and I started to retreat into myself, giving up on the possibility of ever finding Mr Right. Even though I hated being on my own, I began to stay in more, keen to avoid nights out where I would inevitably just face rejection. Somehow, loneliness felt easier to deal with than constant knockbacks. I started to turn down invites from friends and tried to get over the disappointment that my attempt at dipping my toe back into the dating world had been a failure.

So I was still getting used to the fact that I might be single forever when, after a particularly stressful week at the Foundation, I let myself into my flat, kicked off my heels and changed into my PJs. I had brought some work home with me, determined to get on top of it before Monday, and I'd stopped on my way home to pick up some Chinese food and a DVD. I was trying desperately to keep my mood buoyant and not think about being on my own, even though I knew that right now most of my friends would be getting ready for a night on the town. Kay had been texting me all day, asking me to come out that evening, and my phone flashed with a new message from her as I put on some music to fill the silence.

'You sure you don't wanna come out and play? Last chance? xx'

I tapped back, 'Nah, tired and got a take-away now, maybe tomorrow. Have fun xx'

I still hadn't fully furnished the flat and was using an upturned cardboard box as a table, with a deck chair on either side. Very glam! I transferred my take-away food to a plate, set it on top of the box and went to fetch myself a glass of wine. But on my return I stopped short: my dinner was no longer where I had left it.

Confused, I scanned the room, but the plate was nowhere to be seen. Was I going mad? Could it still be in the kitchen? I looked down at the box again and noticed something shining through the gap between the cardboard flaps. I lifted the box, and there in a pile on my carpet was a messy nest of noodles: my plate had slid through and dropped onto the floor. I sat down and stared at it in exasperation for a few minutes, then grabbed my phone and texted Kay.

'Am I too late to come out?'

I was so relieved when she texted right back.

'No, I'll swing by and get you in half an hour.' I'd never got ready so fast.

When Kay arrived, I jumped in her car and told her all about my dinner debacle. We both laughed our heads off and she stopped to buy me some chips for my grumbling tummy.

'See, Katie, it's a sign that you shouldn't be sitting in on your own. The powers that be did it on purpose so you'd come for a drink.'

'It's left a right greasy stain on the carpet. And I was really bloody looking forward to it!'

We laughed again but I knew Kay had a point. I wasn't going to meet anyone sitting at home eating take-away food.

I'd begun to realise that, since I'd made that momentous decision to have another go at dating, I'd first gone out too much, full of enthusiasm, then stayed in too much, to avoid rejection. It had been all or nothing, so now I was determined to strike a balance. I started to go out again and this time tried to lower my expectations, but it was hard, each and every time I applied my mascara or chose what to wear I'd wonder if it would finally be the night for my heart to start healing.

Almost every time Kay and I went out there'd be plenty of guys who'd approach her, and she'd deflect her would-be suitors' advances, explaining that she was engaged but that I was single. But they'd soon disappear. And if someone approached her with a wingman, typically the mate would either talk to me about the attack, or completely ignore me and play on his phone. Charming. It was such a crushing contrast to how my life had been prior to the attack. The old Katie was always chatted up by guys and didn't even have to make an effort to get attention. The old Katie could take her pick of men. The new Katie didn't seem to fit in anywhere.

But Kay, Juliet, Sam and other friends, and my sister Suzy, refused to let me give up. During my recovery, I'd spent so many years staying in and watching box sets on a Saturday night with my dog Barclay on my lap that they reckoned I had a lot of ground to make up. And just because I wasn't having any luck with men didn't mean we couldn't all get a bit merry and have a dance.

One Saturday night Kay convinced me to join her at a new bar near her house in Clapham that she'd been raving about for ages. We'd been there a couple of hours and we had fallen into a deep conversation about what kind of wedding dress she should choose (she was championing the merits of the strapless column, while I waxed lyrical about the bias cut), when a tall, dark-haired guy at the bar caught my eye. At first I ignored him, sure that he was motioning to the girl behind me, but when I went up to get another round, we started chatting and he said his name was Chris. He was much taller than me but I was sure I could feel some chemistry between us, so when he offered to buy me a drink, I accepted.

The three of us spent the rest of the night talking, and when Kay went outside to grab us a taxi, Chris kissed me and we swapped numbers. I was staying the night at Kay's and by the time we got back to her flat, I was giddy, a heady mix of tipsiness combined with the excitement of my first kiss in what felt like forever.

'I can't believe he actually kissed me! I think he really liked me.'

'How exciting! Well, let's see what happens but you could be back in the saddle.' Kay was happy for me, but understandably cautious after all I'd been through with men recently.

'I'm serious, he asked for my number, I've got a really good feeling about this.'

I went to sleep, replaying the kiss in my mind as if I was thirteen and had just come home from the school disco. I pictured his face and him gently leaning in, our lips grazing one another's.

The next day I woke up with a sore head but a smile on my face. I grabbed my phone to check the time and my heart skipped a beat when I saw I already had a text from him.

'Hi, great to meet you last night, I had lots of fun. Let's do it again soon, Chris xx'

We spent the rest of Sunday texting each other. I was sure it was the start of something special.

At work the following day, I could barely concentrate, and over the next week we texted constantly, sending flirty messages and signing off with kisses. I felt like I hadn't done in years – normal; like every other girl my age in a budding romance. Both of us were keen to get together again as soon as we could, so we arranged to see each other the following weekend. On the Friday afternoon, a text from him flashed up on my phone.

'Are you at work? xx'

I grabbed the phone.

'Yep xx'

'I forgot to ask where you work, is it in an office?'

My heart hit the pit of my stomach. It suddenly occurred to me that he might not have realised I was burned, that I was 'that acid girl', as the press sometimes referred to me. I hadn't told him. The pub had been dark except for tea lights on the tables and I'd had my make-up and hair done. All our texts since then had been about things other than work. I thought carefully about how to answer.

'Yeah, I work for a charity in West London.'

'Is it a big one? Would I know it?'

I tried to keep calm.

'You wouldn't have heard of it, it's not very big. The Katie Piper Foundation. It's a burns charity.'

I waited for what seemed like an eternity before my phone beeped with his response.

'Oh my God, have you ever met her?'

My mouth went dry. I scrolled back through all his texts before realising with dawning agony that he'd never referred to me by my name in any of them. I'd introduced myself to him as Kate, something I often did to try and separate the public Katie Piper from the private Kate I was trying to be. I searched furiously for some clue that he knew who I was, but there was nothing. With trembling fingers I typed my reply.

'Ha ha. Yeah, because I am Katie Piper xx'

That was the last I ever heard from him.

I gave him all night to reply before calling Kay the following morning.

'What do you think I did wrong?'

She tried to be reassuring. 'Nothing, Kate, nothing at all.'

'Do you think he had his phone stolen? Do you think that's why he hasn't replied?'

I was desperate for her to give me an excuse I could believe, other than the fact that he just didn't want me. But Kay was always honest.

'No,' she said, 'I don't.'

'Perhaps he doesn't have any phone credit and doesn't get paid until next month?'

Chris had seemed perfect; he was funny, charming, sexy . . .

'I think you should leave it, Kate. I don't think you should text him again.'

I was getting frantic.

'But what if he's had an accident? What if he can't actually physically text me but really wants to?'

I ran through every possible scenario in my mind, and waited anxiously for him to get back in touch. For a week we had been texting each other about eight times a day but now it was complete radio silence. I had got my hopes up so high. His had been the first message I'd received every morning, and texting him was the last thing I'd done every night before I went to sleep, and suddenly that was it. Cut off. Dumped. Rejected.

I took it really hard, mostly because it felt so symbolic. I didn't have a proper night's sleep for weeks afterwards. I'd stare at myself in the mirror, looking at my face from every angle possible, berating myself for even thinking someone could have been into me when there are so many attractive girls to choose from who haven't been burned and aren't disfigured. It was frustrating because, although I was still attracted to guys like Chris, I felt they viewed me totally differently now. I began to think I should lower my expectations, and that I would fare better if I started going for a different kind of man.

I didn't have time to dwell on the situation with Chris much longer, though, as work was keeping me busy. My first book, *Beautiful*, was due to be released in the UK at the start of 2011 and the time had come for the first part of the European book tour that had been arranged for me – I was off to Amsterdam to meet the publishers of the Dutch edition, which was scheduled for release after the UK edition. I was nervous and excited but glad of the distraction. I asked Suzy to come with me and we'd decided to turn it into a girly weekend away.

My meetings with the publisher all went brilliantly. There was lots of interest in me from the media, and in particular from TV companies who wanted to talk to me. So while I was there I pre-recorded some interviews for them which would be aired when the book was finally released.

On our final night I had a surprise up my sleeve for Suzy.

'Why don't we go to the red-light district? It's what Amsterdam is famous for.'

'Kate, seriously?'

I was adamant we should have an adventure.

'Yeah, why not? Come on, it'll be a laugh.'

'Kate, what if you're recognised? You don't want it getting twisted that you were prowling the sex district do you?'

I laughed out loud at the absurdity of the question.

'Suzy, don't be daft. Barely anyone knows who I am back home, let alone here. We'll be completely anonymous. Come on, it'll be a laugh, something to cross off the bucket list.'

We chose a club and were trying to stifle giggles as we waited in the queue to get in, when someone shouted my name.

'Katie? Katie?'

Thinking they were calling out to someone else, I didn't turn, even though the voice had an unmistakeable London accent.

'Katie? Katie Piper?'

An overwhelming sense of embarrassment started to cloak my entire body as I turned and saw the doorman at the front of the queue motioning me towards him, waving and shouting.

'Katie, come through . . . Make way ladies and gents please for Katie Piper. Come on, Katie.'

Suzy stood mute. Grabbing her hand, I dragged her from where she was rooted to the spot and up to the front. The man who'd been calling me shook my hand hard, pumping it up and down as he spoke.

'You're such a strong woman. I saw your documentary. I'd have killed that bastard for what he did to you, love. I'm Pete, pleased to meet you.'

He insisted we were fast-tracked into the club. I opened my mouth to decline his kind offer, not daring to catch Suzy's eye in case we both ended up in fits of laughter. But before I could utter a word, he'd pulled back the curtain over the door and was motioning us inside.

We were ushered in, with the attending bar staff instructed to give us a table and a free drink. After thanking the waiter, I turned to Suzy, about to dissect what had just happened, when a pretty brunette girl rushed up to our table.

'You're Katie Piper, aren't you? I'm Anna, I'm on my hen do with my mates, we're from Leeds and have all seen your documentary, can we get a picture with you?'

I could feel myself flushing and thanked God it was dark in there. While I posed for pictures and made small talk I could see Suzy out of the corner of my eye, doubled up with laughter. As soon as Anna and her friends had gone back to their table, I grabbed Suzy and darted for the exit before the show had even started.

On the way out, we ran into a bunch of guys on a stag do who wanted yet more pictures, before we finally escaped into the cool evening air, feeling overwhelmed at everyone's friendliness. As we leaned against a wall while our laughter subsided, Suzy took the first opportunity to hit me with an I-told-you-so.

'See, I said you'd be recognised, didn't I?'

Thankfully no one I met that night contacted the papers to say I'd been prowling the red-light district, so a few weeks later when *Beautiful* was released, I didn't have to field awkward questions about why I'd been hanging out in such a dodgy area.

The book seemed to strike a chord with so many people and it sold really well right from the beginning. I remember the morning I first saw *Beautiful* on the *Times* bestseller list. It seemed surreal. I knew I had a lot of support from friends and the general public, but enough to get my book to the number one spot in the whole of the UK? I simply couldn't believe it.

Mum and Dad were hugely proud of me and Mum was especially delighted as she is an avid reader and passed her love of books and reading on to me. We'd walk past WHSmith and Waterstones and see the book in the window and I'd want to sneak in and have a look, but didn't want to seem big-headed. Mum had no such fears, and soon she became my PR department in Hampshire. She'd call me every week to tell me she'd been down to Tesco and made sure the bookshelves were fully stocked – she even moved my book around to make sure it had top spot on the bestseller list!

But what really made me smile was not a high position on a sales chart, but hearing or reading people's responses and reviews to *Beautiful*. It made me feel like my story was helping others – which was what I had fundamentally hoped to do when I'd first set out to write the book. The book's success had another, deeper, meaning too. When I had been cross-examined in court during my attackers' trial, the defence lawyers tried to blame me for being raped, somehow suggesting it was my fault, that I should be ashamed, that it should be a secret, not something that should be talked about out loud. Now I felt like my story, the one they'd tried to paint as sordid, was one I could be proud of, and one that could inspire others.

A few weeks after the book's release, Kay and Suzy organised a girls' night out in Putney to celebrate its success and also perhaps to try to boost my confidence in the dating field again. I'd pushed the experience with Chris out of my head because I'd been so busy, but if the truth be told, in quiet moments I would find myself thinking about it and worrying about what went wrong. Despite our last texts having been over a month ago, I still checked my phone occasionally, just in case, even though I knew deep down I wouldn't be hearing from Chris again.

There were five of us girls out that night, and as luck would have it, after a bit of bar-hopping, we met a group of five single guys and ended up hanging out and dancing with them until the small hours. It was completely platonic, but we all got along brilliantly and had a good laugh. In the following weeks, we started to meet up with them regularly on nights out. There was one, Ryan, who I thought was really nice. He was tall with dark hair, piercing blue eyes and he had a kind face with a gentle smile, but my confidence was at rock bottom so he became my secret crush. Left to my own devices I'd never have done anything about it.

But one night Ryan pulled me drunkenly aside from the group and asked if I wanted to go out with him on his own the following weekend. I couldn't believe it and could feel the panic rising. It was never really well-lit wherever we all hooked up so he'd never had a proper look at me; my friends knew I was burned, but did he? He'd never mentioned it but he must have known, mustn't he? The mere thought of Ryan turning out like Chris made me feel queasy. I wasn't sure I could take another rejection, certainly not one so obvious, hurtful and unfeeling as Chris's had been.

Ryan said there was a restaurant in Mayfair he wanted to try and offered to book us a table. I'd hoped we'd go to a pub or somewhere a bit more casual like Nando's, not somewhere quite so formal, so posh, so high-pressure. I was nervous enough about the date, so an exclusive central-London restaurant where people went to be 'seen' was the last place I wanted to go. But I also didn't want to say no, or seem difficult or ungrateful, so we agreed a date and made plans to meet in front of the restaurant at 7pm.

When the day came, I painstakingly went over my hair and make-up. I wanted to feel as good as possible. The clocks had just gone forward and so it wasn't dark yet when I made my way to the restaurant. I cursed myself for agreeing to meet outside and not inside where the dimmed lighting would be kinder. I saw him waiting out front and approached him tentatively. The setting sun was shining full glare, right on my face. I knew every little line would be showing; every wrinkle, every chasm, every crevice, every fold, every shadow. Despite all my make-up, my scars were on full view, as if they'd been put under a microscope.

The minute his eyes landed on me it became painfully awkward and devastatingly obvious I wasn't what he was expecting. He didn't have a clue how I really looked. His mouth hung open, he was visibly shocked and couldn't do anything to hide it. He was silent. I was dying inside.

I broke the ice. 'Hi Ryan.'

'Hi . . .'

His eyes scanned every inch of my face over and over and over again. I knew I had to take charge before complete and utter embarrassment engulfed us both.

I pointed to the door. 'Shall we?'

I tried to sound as bright and breezy as I could, despite the fact my mouth had suddenly gone dry and my hands had started to shake. We went in and he waited while I put my jacket into the cloakroom. Even as I was getting my ticket I could see he was still staring at me. He literally couldn't take his eyes off me, but not in the way any woman wants to be looked at.

We weaved our way to the back of the restaurant where our table was waiting. Everyone was busy with their food and conversations, but I was so self-conscious that it felt like all eyes were on me. Ryan's definitely were. While we looked at the menu we made what I can only describe as the most painful small talk in the history of awkward conversations. I tried to be as light-hearted as possible and kept up a steady stream of let's-make-the-most-of-a-bad-situation chatter. I asked him lots of questions to avoid any crushing silence. He answered my questions robotically, telling me he was a banker and worked in the City. I could just tell he was searching for a way out as quickly as possible.

When I paused to draw breath, he seized his opportunity.

'There are some colleagues I know over there from work. I'm just going to pop over and say hi so I don't look rude. You choose what you want and I'll be back in a minute . . .'

He stood up at such speed he practically sent his chair flying. He'd turned from the nice-guy Ryan I thought I knew into some cold, bumbling bag of nerves, desperate to get away from the disfigured girl and undo the mistake he'd made when he asked me out in the first place.

We'd already ordered drinks, but as I sipped my Diet Coke the waiter kept coming back while I sat there alone, asking if we were ready to order. I waited for what felt like an eternity, trying not to look as worried as I felt.

After twenty-five minutes Ryan still hadn't come back, and by now I'd started to suspect that he wasn't going to. I scanned the restaurant from my seat, trying to find him, but he was nowhere to be seen. I felt hot, sick and embarrassed all at the same time. I wanted to cry, but I managed to calm myself by giving him another five minutes in my head, convincing myself he must be in the toilet. Ten minutes later, having watched four men go into the loos and then come out again, I had to face the fact that he'd left.

Humiliation and nausea washed over me in waves. People had seen us walk in together and now I was about to walk out by myself. I felt paranoid, like everyone was watching me, either laughing at me or cringing for me and saying to themselves, 'That poor girl, as if she hasn't been through enough, now her date has walked out on her.' My lip started to go and I bit it hard to stop the tears. I didn't want to cry but the more I tried not to, the more tears pricked my eyes. My voice wobbled when I asked for the bill and my hands shook as I paid. The coward hadn't even had the decency to leave money with the waiter.

We'd been seated on a raised platform, so everyone could see me as I stood up. I tried to exit as discreetly as I could but tears started tumbling down my cheeks as I made my way back towards the door through the tightly packed tables, head down and alone. Choking back sobs, I collected my coat and rushed out into the cool, fresh evening air. The tears wouldn't stop. Back in the safety of my car, I cried until there were no tears left. I cried out of humiliation, hurt, resentment, but most of all I cried tears of anger at my own stupidity. I'd set myself up *again*. Believed someone could actually like me and be interested in me again. Staring at my scarred, tear-stained face in the rear-view mirror, I felt like an idiot for even thinking it could have been possible.

Chapter Four

Mercifully, not long after my date from hell I was able to shift my attention to something more positive – an awards ceremony for *Red* magazine, who had voted me their 'Woman To Watch'. I was determined nothing would overshadow it, not even Ryan's hideous behaviour. I pushed all the insecurity he had provoked out of my mind, concentrating on the day ahead, not the one behind me.

My agent, Joanne, had told me about a fortnight before the actual event that I'd be getting the award, and when I mentioned I had no idea what to wear to such a prestigious do, she reminded me of Victoria Beckham's very kind offer to lend me a dress. Joanne enquired on my behalf and I was sent the most exquisite teal green dress. It was absolutely beautiful – chic, but comfortable. I loved it and paired it with a statement necklace. It felt amazing to wear a dress I could never have afforded.

The lunch was held at the Saatchi Gallery in Chelsea and it was such an uplifting occasion. I'd been honoured in the past with awards for bravery and survival, but this felt different – it was about my achievements since the attack and what more I might do and give in the future. I was among a group of incredibly accomplished women including Caroline Lucas, the first Green MP in Britain (who won the 'Ethical and Eco' award), Dr Janine Erler, creator of new cancer treatments (recipient of the 'Pioneer' award), and Julia Jones, a leading female conductor who was honoured for her contribution to music. They were all leaders and trailblazers who were known for empowering other women. I couldn't believe my name was among theirs.

Standing on the red carpet on my way in, I felt like everyone believed in me, and that somehow, despite how far I had come already, I still had potential, and so much more to do. It was ridiculously exciting. And it also made me realise that what had happened with Ryan was his total loss.

Any self-doubt I'd had since moving to London on my own seemed to evaporate that day. The award was the affirmation I needed to believe in myself, and in the weeks that followed, I decided to take a break from dating and focus on friends, family and work. *Beautiful* was still on the bestseller lists and I was being contacted daily by people who'd read it to tell me how much they loved it. While I was still susceptible to bouts of loneliness, these were tempered by a full workload and kind passers-by who stopped me in the street or spoke to me at events, like when I spoke at my old junior school in Hampshire about disfigurement and learning to accept differences.

Doing talks like that have always been a good way for me to remind myself to stay strong when life throws social challenges at me. When I stand in front of a room full of strangers, I remember that some people have never listened to a disfigured person or seen them up close, and this is my opportunity to share my experiences with them and help them see that disfigurement is nothing to be frightened of. As they come to a better under-standing of what disfigurement means, the stronger I feel – both as a woman with scars, and as a member of a society who is changing attitudes.

Of course, no matter how confident I may feel on any given day, I'll always be that little bit self-conscious when I see people whisper behind their hands while I'm doing my weekly shop, or when cab drivers slow down and point me out to their passengers. Who wouldn't feel awkward or on show? Some of it might be down to people recognising me but feeling too shy to approach me, but even if that accounts for some of the stares and whispers, often I know I'm simply being stared at because I'm different.

Since the attack I've never been comfortable with having atten-tion called to how I look. In the early days, while I tried to put those kinds of comments down to curiosity, it was hard not to take certain reactions as prejudice, or even just rudeness. On a few occasions people who've had too much to drink have walked right up to me and asked, 'Oh my God, what happened to your face?' One time a guy came up to me while I was waiting for a taxi and said, 'Hi. You're Katie Piper, aren't you?' When I said yes he smiled and replied, 'I just wanted to say, don't worry about being burned; in a weird way it suits you. You look good. Anyway, have a good night, bye.'

I knew he was only trying to be kind, complimentary even, but having my differences pointed out in any way is sometimes hard to hear.

Interviews for my book were still being arranged. Ever since *Beautiful* had first been published, I had been speaking to media from all over the world on a regular basis about my story, which meant I found myself recounting the attack during every inter-view. I had an inkling this wasn't good for my psyche but I couldn't very well refuse to answer questions about the content of the book and still hope to promote it. Unfortunately, the consequence of rehashing these events so intensively was that I started to have flashbacks. I'd speak openly to a journalist and then spend days afterwards having nightmares and horrific memories of my rape. I couldn't just stop talking about it, so all I could do was hope that these feelings and fears would subside when the rounds of press and interviews finally finished. At least, that's what I tried to convince myself whenever I woke up in a cold sweat at 3am.

One evening when I got home from work, kicked off my heels, poured myself a glass of white and logged on to check my email, I saw that I had a message from a woman who explained she was the same age as me and had been living with disfigurement for twenty years, having been burned in a house fire as a child. Her name was Maria, and she told me that she'd felt like there was a glass wall between her and life, and for years she had segregated herself by choice. But now, having seen my documentary and read my book, she'd started taking steps towards integrating herself back into society. She told me that she'd started writing a blog about her experiences and was overwhelmed by the support she was suddenly getting. She now had a Twitter feed with hundreds of followers. She wrote that she'd started applying for part-time jobs, and while she hadn't had any luck so far, seeing what I'd achieved gave her strength to keep trying every day.

I stood at the window in my flat, watching the busy street below, thinking about her words. I could relate so much to what she was saying, about finding her place in the world, and I also thought about the glass walls I had to face too. I printed out Maria's letter and read it over and over. She'd felt hopeless but I'd given her hope; maybe now she could do the same for me?

On the outside, it looked as though things couldn't have been going better for me, but having spent weeks battling with flashbacks and nightmares, on the inside I was a bit of a mess. I decided I'd do what Maria had done – I'd look to others to keep me strong. I spent hours that night reading and re-reading tweets, emails, letters and messages from all the people who'd contacted me to tell me I'd helped them. I'd felt low when I'd come through the door earlier that evening, but by the time I fell asleep I felt like I had when I got my *Red* award. I wished I could thank each and every person who'd written me kind words, who'd made me feel better, stronger, just like Maria said I'd done for her.

Chapter Five

With everything at last appearing to move forward in positive ways, and with the success of *Beautiful*, the press seemed keen to present my life as though it was all wrapped up with a neat bow on top. In their version it all seemed so straightforward; I'd been burned, had treatment, got better, set up my charity, moved to London and was seemingly back on my feet with loads of friends, an exciting life and a good career underway. They'd photograph me on nights out, at awards, industry events or launches, looking happy and carefree.

Seeing these pictures of myself in the papers or in a magazine was still completely surreal. Having my name called out by paparazzi with flashbulbs going off felt bizarre – and still does. I'm just Katie, the same girl I always was. I'd read interviews with people who'd say I was their hero, that I was the person they most wanted to be like, shaking my head in disbelief that they even knew who I was.

Headlines would still call me 'acid girl', something I'd struggled with since my story first hit the papers immediately after the attack, back when I was anonymous. At first it had made me laugh, conjuring up an image of me wearing a cape and pants over my tights like a superhero, with a big 'A.G.' emblazoned on my Lycra chest. But now I was ready to move on from it; to me the label said 'victim' rather than 'survivor' – and I wanted to be the latter. I knew it was an easy way of identifying me, but every story, every award and every picture seemed to describe me like this. If you had Googled those words back then, 'acid girl' would have come up with over ten million hits, mostly about what happened to me. (Though sadly, acid attacks happen often enough that there are too many other girls out there who also fit this tragic description.)

I couldn't change the 'acid attack' part of my headline, because it's written all over my face, but I wanted to find other ways of taking control of my identity and how I was perceived in the media. For a start, I felt that as long as I *looked* like the girl who made *My Beautiful Face*, I would still be *perceived* as a victim. So I reasoned the best way to address this was to change my appearance. I've always been practical and if there's a solution to be found, I'll find it. So, I decided to start at the top – literally.

My hair has always been my calling card; long, blonde and down my back, or bobbed with a thick fringe framing my blue eyes. Other people had identified me by my hair and it was a big part of what made me feel like me. If you had told me then that some day I might change its colour, I'd have laughed in disbelief.

My hair had to be shaved off in the hospital after the attack, and seeing it grow during my recovery brought me reassurance that part of the old me was coming back. When it was finally long enough for me to set, curl and style again, I felt like I'd reclaimed something my attackers had tried to take away from me.

But nearly three years on, I suddenly wanted to get rid of it. I felt it defined me too much, and was a big part of what made me instantly recognisable as 'acid girl'. It wasn't just a hope that the press would see me differently; I felt that changing my hair might mean that people in the street wouldn't recognise me at all, and therefore wouldn't ask me so often about what had happened. And finally, I hoped that maybe the flashbacks would stop once the reflection staring back at me in the mirror looked like a different Katie. It seemed an obvious solution. Besides, I knew that if I didn't like my new 'do, I'd be able to just reverse it. Knowing it wasn't final made it feel more like an adventure, an experiment to find a new Katie, or hide from the old one.

Having spent weeks mulling over a million different colours and hairstyles in magazines, I called my hairdresser, Mikey. He came over to my house one Saturday morning to give me the big transformation. Waiting for the dye to work its magic, I thought about how exciting a 'new me' would be. Four hours later, I'd gone from blonde to pitch black with long extensions down my back. When it was done, I stared at my reflection, both delighted and taken aback in equal measure at how different I looked. For some reason my scars seemed less noticeable. I was so drawn to the darkness that now framed my face that I didn't focus on my skin. I prayed it would be the same for everyone else.

After Mikey left, I spent hours trying different make-up looks. The more I experimented, the more I became convinced that having dark hair made my face look less disfigured. My thick fringe gave me something to hide behind and the long extensions could be pulled over my shoulders, veiling my cheeks. The blonde ex-model in the newspapers was the victim, but this strong, dark-haired woman staring back at me from the mirror was definitely the survivor.

Having jet-black hair was a full-time job, though, between the root touch-ups and the time it took to apply eye make-up that was dramatic enough to work with the hair colour but didn't make my pale skin look overwhelmed. But every minute of maintenance was worth it because my hopes were becoming reality, as I was being recognised much less in public.

My new anonymity actually caused some funny moments, like the time Suzy and I went to a comedy show in Leicester Square. For our evening out I had decided to complement my fringe by wearing thick black eyeliner, which I'd flicked out at the edges. A few minutes into the show, the comedian started asking people in the audience where they were from. He teased a Dutch couple, mocking their accents, and did the same to a group of Americans, who gave as good as they got. Both Suzy and I were laughing hard when his eyes turned towards us. He instantly started pretending to be Chinese before asking me why Chinese people take so many pictures whenever they come to London. I looked around before I realised he meant me! I could see Suzy doubled up laughing. And while I saw the funny side as everyone around laughed with us, I couldn't help but also feel proud that I'd succeeded in becoming a new Katie. I looked different enough not to be treated with kid gloves, not to be given sympathy, not to be stared at and, most of all, not to be recognised. It was brilliant.

But of course, changing myself on the outside didn't completely help me come to terms with who I was on the inside. I'd fixed a symptom, but the root cause of the problem was still lurking.

Shortly after the comedy gig, a middle-aged woman in a business suit stopped me one morning as I was getting in my car to drive to work. She recognised me despite my dark hair. She told me how I inspired her, but I was suddenly overcome with sadness.

'You're amazing, Katie, you really are. You seem like you're stronger now than ever before. How you've dealt with everything, putting them behind bars like you did. You're completely fantastic.'

'I don't know about that but thank you anyway, you're very kind.'

I climbed into my car and put the key in the ignition, waving to her as I drove away. I spent the entire commute trying to figure out who the girl was that she'd been talking about, because it certainly didn't feel like me.

Her words stayed with me throughout my busy day and by the time I got home that night I was emotionally and physically exhausted. I'd barely taken my shoes off when the tears started falling. It was then that it hit me that the pressures, anxieties and unresolved feelings were all really getting to me. I started pleading with the silence for answers.

'People can't know I'm barely coping, people can't know I'm not the survivor I'm supposed to be. That's not who Katie Piper is, that's not who people want Katie Piper to be. You're not the Katie people think you are and you're certainly not the Katie you used to be, so who are you?'

What I did know was that I was the girl who was struggling, who couldn't escape what had happened to her. The girl whose physical wounds were healing but whose emotional wounds still felt raw and painful. The girl who still had nightmares and flash-backs and wanted so badly to forget.

I was terrified to admit that I wasn't what people thought I was, because that left a huge, gaping, imponderable question: who was I really?

Chapter Six

Kay could tell I wasn't doing so well. She'd done her best to bolster my spirits in the aftermath of Chris and Ryan, but she had an inkling I wasn't telling her the whole story. She'd call and could sense I'd been crying, but I'd refuse to say why.

She'd already stood by me as I went to hell and back after the rape and attack, so I didn't feel I could unburden on her any more than I already had. I know now that she wouldn't have minded and that it would have made her feel good to help me, but at the time I didn't want to be the friend that once again needed to be helped. With hindsight I shouldn't have been so proud, not with my best friend.

Kay called me one Friday asking me if I wanted to go out that evening, but I said no, telling her I'd been struggling all week with nightmares and flashbacks that were worse than normal. She reluctantly gave up asking, but then turned up at my flat out of the blue half an hour later, taking charge and declaring that we were going out anyway. I resisted but she wouldn't take no for an answer.

'Kate, come on. You're spending far too much time on your own again. It's not healthy and you know it's not. You need to get out and live a bit more, whether or not you're looking to meet someone.'

She put her arms around me and gave me a squeeze.

'It'll be fun, I promise. Come on, Tiny.'

It was the nickname she'd given me when we first met and she used it whenever she wanted to make me smile. It worked.

We went to one of our favourite pubs and after a while bumped into a group of people we both knew; old mates who were jobbing in TV. One introduced me to his mate, Jake. We had seen one another around enough to say 'hi' to but had never properly spoken.

Jake and I started chatting and were soon flirting with one another. I would never normally have mentioned anything about the attack to a guy I'd only just really met, but I was feeling quite tipsy and after the run of bad luck I'd recently had, I decided to take charge of the situation and make sure he knew I was disfigured rather than leave anything to chance. After some more small talk I plucked up the courage and blurted out, 'You know I'm burned, right?'

His answer was matter-of-fact.

'Yeah.'

I paused: it wasn't the answer I'd expected.

'Oh, okay. I just didn't want you to be flirting with me if you thought I looked like everyone else.'

He gave me a cheeky smile and said, 'I think you look nice.'

I couldn't believe he'd said that, and with a smile on my face we spent hours dancing, and when it was time to go, we swapped numbers.

It was such a fun evening, and the next morning I woke up on cloud nine. I called Kay first thing.

'Kay, he knows I'm burned and said he's not bothered.'

'That's great, Kate. See? I told you.'

'I'm not going to get my hopes up after what's happened but at least there's no big reveal to come.'

Though I didn't hear from Jake straight away we bumped into one another again the following weekend. He came right over and said, 'I've been dead busy but was going to text you. You look great.'

I was relieved.

'Thanks. Don't worry, I've been busy too.'

'I figured you'd be out tonight too. Want another drink?'

I grinned. 'Please.'

Throughout the spring and summer of 2011 Jake and I would see each other every week or so, either finding one another in a local pub or arranging to meet towards the end of the night after we'd been out with friends. We were no Romeo and Juliet, and he wasn't really my type either physically or personality-wise; I thought he was a bit awkward and oddly judgemental as he continually passed comment on strangers. But the fact that he didn't run a mile knowing I was burned was enough for my battered ego to think I should be grateful for the attention and stick with him.

Weekend meet-ups turned into hanging out during the week, just the two of us. The more time we spent together, the more I realised he was wracked with his own insecurities. He would switch from being really needy to being defensive and arrogant. And he wasn't terribly gentlemanly, either. Days would go by without him calling, but then he would turn up without an excuse for the silence. I knew there were real problems but I was too scared to give up on anything that passed for a relationship. I tried to convince myself of reasons why I should like him, but in my heart it didn't feel right.

We'd been seeing each other for a couple of months when I was due to have a graft operation on my eye. The scars on my eyelids had retracted, which meant I could no longer close them properly. I needed the operation to release the skin so I would be able to blink normally and shut my eyes again.

Mum and I had arranged that she would take me to and from the hospital for the outpatient procedure because I wouldn't be able to drive. Plus, she came with me for nearly all my operations. She'd originally planned to stay overnight with me after the op but when we got back to the flat my phone beeped with a text from Jake, asking if he could come over. I was suddenly desperate to see my new-ish boyfriend and send Mum away.

'Mum, I'll be fine, you go. Jake's coming over in a minute to see me anyway. He can get me anything I need.'

She gave me a long look. 'I don't think I should go, Kate. You've only known Jake a few months. Why don't I stay and then I can help you get sorted in the morning?'

'I'm fine, honestly. You've done enough. Go home to Dad.'

She dug her heels in.

'Kate, I'd really rather stay. I think it'd be better for me to look after you, not Jake.'

I started to get annoyed at my poor mum, who was only trying to help.

'Mum, I don't need to be looked after. Jake can bring me anything I need. Please. Just go home. Now. Stop fussing around me. I'll be fine, I promise. I'll call you in the morning. Okay?'

She eventually relented, kissing me on the top of my head before letting herself out.

I should have listened to her.

I texted Jake, asking him to bring crisps and some bread for toast the next morning. Three hours later, I was still waiting. I sent him six text messages asking where he was and he didn't respond to any of them. I got into bed and tossed and turned for what felt like hours before eventually falling into an emotional sleep.

At 3am the doorbell rang. I sat bolt upright, instantly panicking that someone was trying to break in and kill me. I held my breath, praying it wouldn't happen again, when my phone beeped into life with a new text message.

'Sorry I didn't come round earlier. I'm outside now if you're still awake? Jake xx'

I was so angry that I ignored him, but in a series of lame, drunken texts he said he'd run into mates on the way to mine and had ended up in the pub, and then a club. He was sorry but he had a bottle of wine with him if I fancied sharing it (though he'd neglected to get the crisps and bread).

Eventually I just turned my phone off. He didn't ring the bell again. I lay there in the dark, furious, trying to get back to sleep. I was upset and disappointed in myself as much as I was in Jake. Mum was right. I couldn't rely on him, and letting me down right after my operation was pretty unforgiveable. I spent a wakeful night debating whether it was better to date a loser or not to date at all.

Mum called in the morning to check I was okay. She asked the inevitable.

'Did Jake take care of you?'

There was no way I could tell her the truth after I had sent her away.

'Yeah, he was great. He came right over. Listen, sorry if I was rude. I just. . .'

'Don't worry, Kate. I should have trusted your judgement more.'

I felt terrible for lying to her.

'Mum?'

'Yes.'

'Sorry. I really am. I love you, thanks for taking care of me.'

'I love you too, Kate.'

The following week, after a heart-to-heart, Jake and I decided it was time to part and keep our relationship as mates. There'd never been much invested romantically for either of us, so the split wasn't particularly heartbreaking. Deep down, I had always known we weren't going to last. He'd been what I thought I needed at the time – someone who knew I was burned but who didn't care. But in the aftermath of our split I realised that was only half the battle. Yes, I needed someone who could look past my scars and not judge me by them, but I also wanted someone who adored me, someone who would put me above everyone and everything else. Someone who, right now, it seemed I could never and would never find.

Chapter Seven

With my love life in tatters and loneliness threatening to over-whelm me once again, I decided that what I needed was a bit of distance from my troubles and my day-to-day routine, to help me kick-start the changes I knew I needed to make. As soon as the bandages came off my eye the following week, I began thinking about getting away for a while to find some perspective.

With amazingly good timing, my big brother Paul invited me to stay with him and his fiancée Leah for a week at their place in Colorado. I jumped at the chance. Paul had an executive IT job over there, and his life was so busy that he hadn't been home since the previous Christmas, so it was ages since I'd seen him. He's always been a good influence on me; he somehow manages to calm all my worries. His patience, quiet determination and inner confidence seem to seep into me whenever I'm with him. I completely idolise him, and I couldn't wait to spend some quality time with him and think a little less about my own recent events. I was also looking forward to hearing all about their wedding plans; he and Leah had set a date for September 2012, and Suzy and I were going to be bridesmaids.

I checked my diary and worked out that I could go for ten days. I had a workshop for burns survivors I'd been planning for months that was scheduled for the day I was intending to come back, but I figured I could sleep on the overnight flight home and land ready for work.

I was excited about seeing Paul and Leah, but I was also filled with trepidation about the journey. I'd never been to America, nor flown on my own that far. But, just as I'd known when it was time to move out of my parents' house, I knew now that I had to push myself again and be brave enough to do things that were outside my comfort zone.

When departure day finally came, I nervously checked in at Heathrow, stocked up on magazines for the journey, and found my seat on the plane. Paul had called me a couple of days beforehand to warn me that US Immigration could be pretty ruthless. He told me to smile sweetly, answer all their questions and accept the fact that they might be intrusive and throw their weight around. From the minute we left the tarmac in London I dreaded what they might ask me. After all, I was travelling with a veritable pharmacy; all my post-op medications, eye drops, ointments and creams were in my hand luggage for the flight. I had a separate doctor's letter for each tub and bottle, saying that I was permitted to travel with that volume of liquid because it was for medical treatment. It got me through security at Heathrow so I hoped that wouldn't cause any trouble on the other side.

By the time I landed in Colorado fourteen hours later, I was nervous, sweaty and exhausted. I'd spent most of the flight being sick; the acid I swallowed during the attack left me with scar tissue which constricts my airway and throat, so I have to take small bites when I eat or my food gets stuck down there or gets thrown up again, and for some reason – maybe nerves – I just couldn't eat properly on the plane. But at last we arrived and shuffled off the plane, and I headed for passport control. A stern-faced, suited-and-booted immigration officer eventually called me forward.

He wasted no time.

'What happened to your face?'

Paul had told me to be prepared, but I was shocked at the bluntness of his question.

'Oh, I . . . I got burned . . .'

'How?'

I lowered my head, looking up at him through my fringe like it might protect me. Why did he need to know this?

'It was a chemical injury.'

'What chemical?'

'Acid . . .'

'What, in a laboratory?'

It was relentless.

'No, no, my ex-boyfriend threw acid in my face.'

'No way, where is he now?'

I wasn't happy making small talk about what had happened to me, particularly with so many other people within earshot, but I had no choice but to answer.

'He's in prison.'

'You should be more careful in the future, lady.'

As if I needed that advice . . .! He stamped my passport and waved me through. I walked away feeling that all he'd wanted from me really was a good story to tell later in the staffroom. As I made my way towards baggage reclaim, I could see people nudging one another and pointing at me. I felt a pang in my chest and rising humiliation.

When I finally reached the arrivals hall, Paul was there waiting for me. He waved and rushed over to hug me. It was the physical pick-me-up I needed. I dug deep and put on my happy face.

'Hey, you look fantastic, Paul! Where's Leah?' I scanned the crowd.

'She's waiting for us in the car. You okay, Kate?' He looked at me with brotherly concern. 'You look really pale.'

'Yeah, yeah, I'm fine. Just knackered, it was a long flight.'

'How was passport control? They can be little power junkies sometimes. Did they stop you?'

I didn't want him to worry, so I fibbed.

'No it was fine. They were good. Maybe it was my smile.'

Paul had arranged to work from home that week, so during the day I'd lie by his swimming pool reading and then he'd take me for dinner in the evening. A few days into my stay, he was driving us somewhere in the car when he glanced over at me.

'I can't wait to get you all back here for the wedding, I'm so glad you're coming over for it. You and Suzy will make amazing brides-maids. How's everything with *your* love life anyway? Found a guy you could see yourself ending up with?'

His question blindsided me and I didn't know what to say. I tried my best not to cry but tears started pouring down my cheeks, and my voice broke as I answered him.

'I feel like no one wants me, Paul. I can't meet a guy, not a decent one who wants me once he's seen me in the cold light of day.   I feel like I'll never be happy; never get married; never have children. Men see me as damaged goods. Since I moved to London I've had one disaster after another.'

His face fell and he did his best to comfort me.

'Ouch. Wow. Ahh, they will, Kate. Don't be silly. You'll meet someone, you will. Don't worry about it.'

He gripped the steering wheel and checked the rear-view mirror. I knew he was struggling to find a way to talk me round on this one. I felt terrible that I was making him feel awkward. I busied myself looking in my handbag for a tissue so our eyes wouldn't meet. But right there, in his car on that freeway in Colorado, I wanted to confess everything. I wanted to tell him how I felt like a joke, how I felt like I was close to having a break-down. I wanted to tell him I was so heart-breakingly, soul-crush-ingly lonely that it consumed every thought in my head, all day long. I wanted to tell him I was terrified of ending up completely alone. Terrified that my attackers had won, that they had succeeded in leaving me unloveable, and that putting on a brave face for everyone was getting harder and harder to do.

Paul did his best to say the right, brotherly thing. 'You'll be okay, Kate, really.'

I looked at him and chickened out, doing my best to put on that brave face yet again. 'God, yeah, I don't know what's wrong with me. You're right, of course I'll be fine. You know me, dramatic old Kate. Anyway, where are we going for lunch?'

Chapter Eight

Despite my wobble in the car, my time with Paul helped recharge my batteries, and some of his confidence and determination rubbed off on me, as I'd hoped it would. Plus, I trusted Paul; so if he told me I was going to be fine, then maybe – just maybe – I would be. Back at the airport on my way home, I waved goodbye and headed to the departure lounge feeling tenfold stronger than when I'd arrived.

Even though I'd intended to sleep on the long journey home, I only managed to snatch about an hour's rest during the whole eighteen-hour journey from Paul's house in Colorado to London via Washington. So by the time I arrived at my flat I was absolutely exhausted and suffering jetlag. I longed to go to bed but my workshop was starting at 10am. Telling myself I'd sleep afterwards, I stopped at the supermarket on my way back home to buy three cans of a five-hour energy drink that claimed to be stronger than Red Bull.

I showered and paced around a bit while I drank my first 'pick-me-up', before heading to the venue to prep the room for the workshop, putting up posters and setting out tables and chairs.

My friend Sam is a professional hairdresser and arrived just after me, having promised he'd help pamper the women who were attending. He caught me as I was drinking my second energy drink and warned me it was strong stuff . . . He was right.

I was wobbling like a half-baked custard by the time the workshop started, high on a mix of adrenaline, caffeine and sleep deprivation, but despite all that it ended up being one of the best workshops the Foundation has ever done. There was a great turnout, including many new attendees who'd never been to one of our events before, and everyone got on really well. New bonds and friendships were forged, phone numbers and email addresses were swapped, and we taught lots of people about camouflage make-up.

By the time the workshop finished, I was so happy but also so exhausted that I could hardly speak. Sam and me walked home with all our kit, and I snuggled up on the sofa with a blanket and the TV remote in my hand. As I wound down, I thought about how the success of the workshop and sharing the day with so many great people had pumped me full of good feelings, and it made me realise that maybe a boyfriend wasn't the most important thing in life. Maybe all I needed was a closeness with other people. Maybe I could be fulfilled, could be happy and could enjoy life with or without a man.

Once I'd recovered from my jetlag, I decided to channel all the positive messages I had learned from the workshop and focus on the future in three ways: I'd park my dreams of finding a man and let myself just be Katie for a while; I'd throw myself into work, which was the one thing I could always rely on to make me feel better about myself; and I'd find a way to deal with the nightmares and flashbacks that were plaguing me.

First, I decided to try and tackle the memories of the attack. I contemplated going back to a psychotherapist, but because discussing the attack constantly in interviews was what I thought had caused the flashbacks in the first place, I was terrified that talking about it further could actually make things worse. It was ironic, because I was always telling people about the merits of therapy, and it had helped me so much in the past, but for some reason when looking after myself this time, I got stuck. Or maybe I was just being stubborn. Either way, I wanted to find an easy way out, a quick fix that would help me forget everything. I know now that this wasn't the way to handle it and I wish I could go back in time and tell myself to do it the right way, but back then, I was still struggling to figure out how to heal myself without having to rehash the past.

Over the next two months I tried just about every alternative therapy I could find. I even investigated Electric Convulsive Therapy (ECT). I had stumbled upon it while Googling ways to erase memories. Electric currents are sent through the brain to relieve major depression and other debilitating psychiatric conditions. Extreme as it may sound, that's how desperate I was to clear my head. Memory loss was possible but not guaranteed, and most people would hope to avoid it, but all I wanted was some relief from the hideous, terrifying memories of what had happened to me. Another internet check and I realised skin burns were also a possible side effect, so I dismissed it instantly and shuddered at the thought of anything that could burn me being attached to my head. I thought it was unjust that the treatment that could potentially rid me of my awful memories of being burned could result in my being burned again. But in truth, it would never have happened anyway. ECT is a last-resort therapy for people who suffer far more extreme psychological disorders than what I was going through, even taking my horrific flashbacks into account, and so it wouldn't have been appropriate for me anyway.

I decided to give hypnotherapy a shot, which is a far more gentle and mainstream approach, and is all about the power of suggestion. I liked the idea of being 'instructed' to forget my memories. I thought I'd start right at the top and tried to make contact with Paul McKenna; I couldn't find a way of reaching him directly so I got in touch with his publishers and asked them to pass on my details, telling him I wanted to see him as a private client. Unfortunately I never heard anything back. I could have asked my agent, Joanne, to make contact on my behalf, but I was trying to keep my work and private lives separate as much as I could, so I didn't want to alarm her by admitting that I needed help.

I rationalised that Mr McKenna was probably just really busy and that maybe I'd hear from him when he eventually had a spare second, so I decided to try meditation in the meantime. If I could learn to meditate and take my mind elsewhere when I had a nightmare or flashback, I could therefore learn how to be in control of my mind, rather than it being in control of me. My friend Lizzy, who swore by meditation, lent me lots of books and CDs. Determined to make a proper effort I set aside an evening to try it all out, put on some leggings and a comfy T-shirt (the most Zen-like outfit I could find) and settled down, cross-legged on the floor, leaning against the sofa. I tentatively pressed play on the first CD.

'Clear your head of all thoughts . . .'

I instantly started thinking about everything. 'What should I have for tea? Would it be warm enough tomorrow to go to work without a jacket? Was the washing still in the machine? What time did *The X Factor* start?'

Clear your head . . . .

'I must remember to send that fundraising thank-you email.'

Clear your head, Kate.

'I think I'll go for coral nails at my manicure tomorrow.'

Clear. Your. Head. Kate!

'Don't forget to tell Mum and Dad you'll be there for lunch on Sunday, and remember to pick up a treat for Barclay.'

Oh, forget it.

Dismayed, but at least having made a decision about my dinner (cheese on toast) I decided to stop and try again another time. Over the next week I persevered, attempting the whole exercise several more times, but I could never get any peace or quiet in my mind. Every time I tried to clear the damn thing, it seemed to go into overdrive.

After that, I gave up on alternative therapies. I took acting classes for a little while, to help improve my confidence and to meet new people. I thought that maybe I could just 'act' when people asked about what had happened to me. I'd still be able to tell my story, but I would learn to recite it verbatim as if it were a scene from a play or film, rather than actually feeling it and reliving it every time I talked about it. I'd be able to maintain the polite Katie who never shied away from a question, but at the same time I wouldn't be leaving my emotional side so open to the nightmares afterwards.

The acting classes did help give me confidence and they certainly kept me busy. I was no Scarlett Johansson but I enjoyed them nonetheless. As an added extra, I also hoped they'd be useful for future TV presenting, if I got the chance. The excitement of filming *My Beautiful Friends* had given me a huge buzz, and I hoped so much to make more programmes that would help people or be educational. I had great plans for the future, if I could just get the past under control.

Chapter Nine

In the summer of 2011, a few weeks after I got back from Paul's, I got a great surprise. My agent, Joanne, contacted me and said that Channel 4 had been in touch and wanted a meeting. They had told me immediately after the original documentary and *My Beautiful Friends* that they wanted to work with me again, but now it was actually happening and they were calling me in to discuss it. It looked like my hopes were becoming a reality!

The night before the meeting, I chose an outfit and laid it out ready. As I brushed my teeth and climbed into bed, I prayed the next day would bring good news. In fact, what it brought exceeded all my expectations when they offered me a two-year contract to be one of their presenters. I was thrilled. I called Mum and Dad immediately to share the news and tell them everything before it went public.

'Hi Mum, guess what?' I was practically jumping up and down.

'What love? Is everything okay?'

'Put the phone on speaker, I want Dad to hear at the same time.'

'Kate, is everything all right?

I could hear the click as they turned on the speakerphone.

'Are you both there? I've got a job at Channel 4.'

There was silence. Then Dad spoke, tentatively.

'What do you mean, a job?'

'I mean I've signed a deal to work for Channel 4. What do you mean, "what do I mean?"'

'What, to work in the offices? That's great news. Well done love, we're really proud of you. What will you be doing exactly?'

Despite the fact that they couldn't see me, I rolled my eyes like a teenager.

'No, Dad, to make TV shows.'

They paused, before speaking in unison.

'*What*?'

I couldn't help but laugh. Mum and Dad always believed in me but this was beyond their wildest dreams too, so it was no wonder they were struggling to get their heads around it.

'Seriously! They want me to make TV shows for them. I'm not temping or filing. I'm not making tea, I'm making TV!'

I spent the next half an hour talking them through exactly what it meant and what I'd actually be doing. News spread through the Piper telegraph to the rest of the family pretty quickly. Suzy texted to congratulate me, and Paul called as soon as he heard, reminding me that he'd said everything would be okay. It meant so much when he then told me he was proud of me.

If I thought I was excited about the possibility of a career in television, that was nothing compared with what my parents were feeling – mostly because of the financial security and stability it would provide me with for the next couple of years at least. Before I moved to West London, Dad wanted me to stay in Hampshire and do something safe and steady like getting a casual retail job.

It's not that he thought I wasn't capable of having a career, but he felt I'd been through enough trauma and didn't need the stress and strain of a difficult or exhausting job.

A few weeks later, I attended the first production meeting at the Channel 4 offices. The developments we discussed left me so stunned that I had to call my parents again straight after.

'They don't want me just to do documentaries about burns and disfigurement or what happened to me, Mum, they want me to make all kinds of programmes with them . . .'

'Oh, Kate, that's fantastic. We're so proud of you.'

It meant so much to all of us that I was being taken seriously for what I can *do*, rather than what I'd been *through*.

That month I barely had a second to myself. Between meetings with the TV teams, outpatient appointments at the hospital to check my eye graft, and writing a lot more for newspapers and magazines, I struggled to fit everything in. But throughout, I remained adamant about my commitment to the Foundation. If I had to take an afternoon or a morning off for other work, I'd make up for it at the office in the evening or over the weekend.

By this time, the Foundation was receiving tens of thousands of emails a week from all over the globe. *Beautiful* had been translated into seven languages, and people from across the world, from India to Africa, America to Australia, were getting in touch to offer personal support and donations to the Foundation. Our database of supporters and donors had trebled in size. Just keeping up with all the correspondence was now a full-time job.

The success of the Foundation was snowballing fast and we predicted we'd treble our 2010 income by the end of 2011. We'd grown to a team of three, and had put together a firmly structured five-year business plan. We were all working long and hard at keeping the charity moving forward. I was getting into the habit of taking packed salads and sandwiches to work so I could have both lunch and dinner at the office, to make up for the time I was taking out for TV stuff. I had a workshop to plan in London for ten survivors and was busy writing letters to cosmetic firms asking for camouflage make-up samples to show workshop attendees, as well as catching up on correspondence and emailing all the trustees with updates.

Working such long days, I had to acknowledge one of my physical limitations: having sight in just one eye is hard enough at the best of times, but when you stare at a screen for hours on end and it starts to tire, you don't have another eye to rely on, and I was subjecting my eye to full-on, ten-hour, screen-filled days.

On one evening I got home and my head was pounding and my eyes were watering. I couldn't stand the thought of watching TV or reading; my working eye was begging me to rest. I changed into my pyjamas and went straight to bed.

Lying there in the dark with my head thumping, despite the painkillers I'd taken, I longed to restore some vision to my blind eye. I hated not being able to judge light and shade, not being able to perceive depth or see a silhouette. I resolved to find out everything I could about the possibility of getting my sight back. I let myself dream there was a chance I could regain at least some of my sight.

For the next few nights I spent hours researching on the internet, watching YouTube documentaries about vision, wading through websites to learn as much as I could about scientific advancements, and finding success stories of people who'd had their sight restored. But I couldn't find anyone in the UK who'd gone on to see after being blinded with acid.

Then I came across a reference to a doctor named Mr Sheraz Daya. I remembered his name from a news piece I'd seen three years before, when I was recovering at home immediately after the attack. His clinic had restored a person's sight using stem cells from a generous organ donor who had died. Stem cell transplants are cutting-edge science, and involve implanting the donated cells directly into the living person's eye. Once inside, the stem cells stimulate the recipient's dormant cells into action, and once the recipient's own cells have 'woken up', they kill off the donor cells and begin regenerating and multiplying, which should eventually result in restored sight.

I Googled Mr Daya and discovered that in the time since I'd first come across him, he'd helped many more people regain their sight in one or both eyes. He seemed to me to be a sight-giving angel. I called his clinic the next day and made a hopeful appointment for the following month.

At our initial consultation, Mr Daya told me that the process wasn't a quick fix. First, my eyelids needed some tweaking to get them ready for this specialised operation. The scar tissue had retracted again, something I was used to, but it meant the lids weren't offering enough protection to my eyes. Once this was fixed, though, he and his team could give the transplant a go. He had to manage my expectations but his next words made my heart skip a beat.

'Once you're ready for the operation, we'll likely be able to restore some sight, but I can't tell you how much.'

Even 'some' sight seemed to me considerably better than none. His enthusiasm for his work was infectious and it gave me great confidence in him.

It turned out that Mr Daya was a colleague of my incredible eye surgeon, Mr Naresh Joshi, who had skilfully reconstructed all of my eye area after the attack.

I am a bit like a patchwork doll around my eyes; all the working parts having been taken from other parts of my body. The skin under my eyes used to be behind my ears, my upper eyelids used to be my groin, and the inside of my eyelids are made from grafts taken from inside my bottom lip, which left a scar that I always chew when I'm nervous or embarrassed. Mr Daya said that between them, he and Mr Joshi would get me ready for the stem-cell operation.

Not long after, Mr Joshi performed another release operation on my lids, and Mr Daya was satisfied that he could now schedule the surgery. A date was set for 7 November for my stem-cell transplant.

The whole process of regaining sight is hugely fascinating, and it wasn't just me who was getting interested. Everyone I talked to about it wanted to know more. How would it work, what would happen, just how much would I be able to see afterwards, and what exactly would the operation entail? In fact, a few days after one of my appointments with Mr Daya, I had a production meeting at Channel 4. We were throwing around lots of ideas for new programmes, but the commissioner, David, kept asking me what was going on outside of work.

'I'm trying to get my sight back in my left eye.'

'Seriously? How would that work? Tell us more.'

I told him about how stem-cell transplants work and how I'd been prepared for the operation.

Then he asked, 'How about we document and follow your progress, Katie? I think it'd bring in a younger audience to science than it traditionally has.'

I still wasn't getting it.

'Pardon?'

'Basically, I think it'd make an amazing documentary. The procedure sounds incredible, it'd show the public another side to your recovery. And it would demonstrate some big advances in medicine. The fact that you're going through the actual process adds another layer to the show, gives it a real human-interest angle.'

Before I knew it, *Katie: The Science of Seeing Again* had been commissioned. I was enthused and excited about the project in a different way to my previous programmes. It engaged me and was giving me a chance to learn more and challenge my mind. *My Beautiful Face* had been all about me and my recovery, and *My Beautiful Friends* was about disfigurement, something I knew a lot about and had first-hand experience of, but this would be about a procedure I still knew very little about. This time, it'd be my job to research the subject fully, to understand it well enough to interview the experts and report the science behind it to the viewer. It was so exciting.

We arranged a meeting the following week to hammer out the filming details. I was desperate to prove I could do a good job and knuckled down fast, reading everything I could. The programme would take me to the US, where stem-cell research is considered highly controversial, largely because of the use of embryonic cells in some cases. I'd meet professors and clinicians, as well as protestors and lobbyists, to show both sides of the argument, which would hopefully dispel some of the fears and myths surrounding the issue. Then I'd come back to the UK and have the operation.

Studying night after night in my little flat, I didn't have the time to feel lonely. I had too much to learn and revise. Crib notes covered my fridge and bathroom mirror so I could learn the facts while I fixed dinner or brushed my teeth. I was determined to get it right, to prove to Channel 4 that they'd done the right thing by giving me a contract. I wanted to show them, myself and everyone else that Katie Piper could be a bonafide documentary maker.

Chapter Ten

The TV commission wasn't the only exciting thing going on in my life at that time. The success of *Beautiful* had led to a three-book deal with a new publisher and I was getting ready to start work on the first one. *Things Get Better* was to be my self-help book on recovery, which was to be followed by a collection of positive affirmations, *Start Your Day with Katie*, to be published shortly after. I had diaries full of affirmations and mantras that I'd used daily during my recovery, had written notes to myself about coping mechanisms and strategies I used in the darkest hours of despair when I was recovering at home or in hospital. The thought of being able to share these with people who needed strength made me feel incredibly proud. Both of these projects were from Katie the survivor, not Katie the victim, and it all felt good. I hoped they would make a difference.

With my days getting longer and fuller, and more and more commitments creeping into my diary, I was able to go home and see Mum and Dad less and less. Spending nights back at theirs like I had when I moved to London was now a thing of the past. Much as I wanted to, I didn't have the time now to sit in traffic and commute to and from Hampshire any more, and my flat was five minutes from the charity's office.

I'd try to make it back for Sunday lunch as often as I could, but knowing Mum and Dad missed me as much as I missed them, I had to make sure that I snatched every opportunity I could to spend time with them. So when I was invited to the Women of the Year Awards in October 2011, I proudly took Mum as my date. There was nobody I wanted to share it with more.

When we arrived we went to have a peek backstage. We'd only been there a few minutes when I heard someone call my mum's name.

'Diane? Diane?'

We both turned round, wondering who could be calling her when I was sure I was the only person there she knew. Weaving her way towards us through an assembled throng of impressive women was Lorraine Kelly. I'd met her several times but Mum had only met her once or twice, but despite that, Lorraine still remembered her name.

She embraced us both and asked Mum at length about how she was and what she'd been up to, asking after Dad too. We made small talk before Lorraine excused herself to get ready to present. We were both so impressed and I know it made Mum feel special. Lorraine Kelly is one of the most honest and sincere people I've met in the media. She really gives her time to her guests and her fans, makes them feel at ease and she always remembers them, no matter what walk of life they come from.

The awards started and as ever I was in awe of the women whose company I was in, such as six military medical personnel including nurses, physiotherapists and a Surgeon Commander who worked both on the battlefield in Afghanistan and at UK rehabilitation centres to help soldiers injured in the line of duty. I also met Nawal El Saadawi, an 80-year-old writer, trained doctor and women's rights activist from Egypt who endured death threats, incarceration and physical attacks for speaking out against female genital mutilation, but who wouldn't be silenced even in her ninth decade. They were all incredibly inspiring, empowering and selflessly generous women.

Part-way through the programme of events, Pam Warren walked onto the stage. Pam had suffered severe burns in the Paddington rail crash in 2000. It was great to see her up there; we had spent some time together during my recovery, three months after my attack. At the time I was too petrified to go out and pain-fully embarrassed by what was left of my face, so she came to visit me at home in Hampshire and subsequently became a bit of a mentor to me. I hadn't spotted her when we were backstage earlier, so I planned to say hi to her after the lunch.

But then Pam announced to the audience that she was there to give the Women of the Year 'You Can' Award. While she was intro-ducing it she found my face in the crowd and to my extreme shock, she announced that it was me who had won. I nearly spat out my drink when she called my name. I looked across at Mum, who was just as shocked as I was. Trembling as the applause grew, I navigated my way through the tables and up onto the stage.

As Pam hugged me and handed me my award, memories flashed through my mind of that first time we met. She'd held my gaze and showed me pictures of her burns, which were just as bad as mine, and told me about her recovery. She was honest with me about the thousands of hours I'd have to spend in the mask and the initial discomfort I should expect from the compression garments, but I could see for myself how the mask and compression garments had worked for her.

She was an inspiration to me when I needed one; she was campaigning for rail safety, running her own business and had a boyfriend. Her success resonated in my mind and found a place in my heart that I've called on countless times since. She gave me hope that I could eventually return to work and function just like everyone else again.

Now here we were, three years later, both of us having moved forward with our lives, as she presented me with an award I'd never have dared dream about. It was an incredibly moving afternoon, made even more poignant by the fact it was also International Women's Day. I was humbled to have my name mentioned alongside my fellow award winners, all world-changing women. It left me feeling stronger and more full of self-belief than ever since leaving my parents' home.

I'd also been feeling much stronger since I'd started to write my self-help book *Things Get Better*. Going back through all my old notes and diaries I'd been reminded of the lessons and tools I'd used to help me recover the first time around, and once again they helped me cope, and the nightmares and flashbacks I'd been having disappeared, replaced by positivity, inspiration and self-belief.

With my confidence returning, I knew that the best thing I could do was to keep moving forward, to believe that things would get better. With this enforced positivity in my heart and mind a few days later, I embarked on my next new adventure – travelling to the US to start filming *The Science of Seeing Again*.

But while the dream of getting my sight back was coming true, I reflected on the fact that the only reason I needed the procedure in the first place was because of the most horrific thing that ever happened to me. As the flight took off and we climbed high above London, I wrote in my diary:

28 October 2011

I'm on the plane flying to Minneapolis. I'm becoming more excited about my stem-cell operation on 7 November – the thought of beating one of the final lasting injuries of the attack is out of this world. Out of the plane window I can see a warm red sunset. It's almost pink.

It's strange to think my journey, my fate in life, has brought me here. The film crew are a few seats in front of me – nowadays I feel so independent – it's weird how half of me prefers to be alone and yet the other half of me is chronically lonely.

Eight hours later, we touched down. I spent the entire time in the queue for passport control praying they wouldn't humiliate me in front of my colleagues like they had done when I visited Paul – I wasn't sure I'd be able to keep it together if they did. But this time around it was much easier.

They called us forward, one by one. When it was my turn, I drew back my shoulders and held my head high.

'Why are you here?'

'We're filming a documentary.'

'You got your permit?'

It felt like an eternity while he pored over my work visa that was attached to my passport. I knew the team had made sure every piece of paperwork was correct and in place, but I couldn't help but hold my breath the entire time.

'Go on through, good luck. I hope it goes well.'

I was stunned by his hospitality.

The crew and I headed towards the carousel to get our luggage and I beamed to myself – I was back in the US but it wasn't like last time when I was travelling by myself, scared, and running away from problems at home. This time I was Katie Piper: documentary maker. And it felt amazing.

Chapter Eleven

Our first interview was with Dr Doris A. Taylor at the University of Minnesota's Center for Cardiovascular Repair. She and her team are world-leaders in stem-cell research and were exploring its possibilities and uses in all fields of science. At the time they were renowned for having recreated a beating rat's heart in a test tube. They had taken the heart of a dead rat and stripped it of its cells, leaving the tough protein structure behind. They then introduced stem cells from infant rats before charging the recipient with electricity and quite literally bringing it back to life. Though it may sound like crazy science from the future, being able to build new organs could be one of the greatest advancements in our lifetime for transplant treatment across the world. The whole process fascinated me and I loved studying it and Dr Taylor's work before we went out there to film. I was proud that, even though I had only got an E in GCSE science, I was about to interview a superstar scientist.

Dr Taylor's work was considered controversial because of her use of embryonic stem cells and because she tested on animals. She'd been threatened by people who opposed her methods, and her laboratory had been broken into and vandalised many times, but she believed deeply in her work and what good it could do in the future. Her focus and determination was inspiring.

We filmed her showing me some of the organs her team had grown in the lab: beating hearts, regenerated livers. She also told me she was trying to grow skin, which would be a game-changing breakthrough for burns survivors. After we'd finished filming, she quizzed me about the Foundation and what we were working on. I explained to her that I wanted to bring the treatment I'd had in France to the UK and make it available for every burns survivor in the country. She took my hands in hers and looked me in the eye.

'Katie, never give up on what you know to be true. You believe in this, and you have to keep campaigning for it.'

We spoke a little while more, and she told me she'd never married or had children. Her work was her life and she'd sacrificed everything for it, but she had no regrets. It reinforced the feelings I was having that I could have a fulfilled life even if I never found my Prince Charming.

As I was leaving she picked up a framed postcard on her desk and handed to me. On it was written, 'Trust your crazy ideas'. She said to me, 'Katie, someone gave this to me, now I want to give it to you.' I was so unbelievably touched I didn't know what to say. I thanked her and promised to cherish it, which I have. Both the message on the card and having had it given to me by Dr Taylor have stayed close to my heart. I felt so lucky for having spent some time with her.

As we drove to the airport for our next destination, I thought about how much I loved my job and all the fascinating people I got to meet, from all walks of life, and how much I was learning from each new encounter.

We were going to Mississippi, the heart of the Deep South, to meet and film anti stem-cell protesters. The programme needed to present a balanced view of the treatment I was going to have, so we were staining them the opportunity to share their opinions. The protesters are generally highly religious people who take particular issue with obtaining stem cells from embryos because their belief is that life begins immediately at conception. They don't condone using this treatment under any circumstances, even if it has the potential to cure painful, incurable or life-threatening diseases that can destroy lives and families. The irony is that their protests sometimes turn violent, and there are some protesters serving time in prison for stalking and killing abortion practitioners.

For the film, I attended a church meeting and followed the congregation on their way to a protest both against stem-cell treatment and against abortion. It was about as pro-life as you could get, with a lot of anger, shouting and propaganda. In the group was a gynaecologist who, surprisingly, was also protesting on the rally. She admitted to me that she discouraged her patients from having abortions on religious grounds, and had even strongly persuaded the parents of a pregnant eleven-year-old girl who had been raped by a family member that she should carry the child to term. I was staggered and tried to phrase my questions with as much journalistic impartiality as I could muster.

'Don't you think the family should have been allowed to make their own decision?'

I was asking direct and pointed journalistic questions to people I would not normally dare challenge, but it was my job to ask the questions the viewer wanted answered. I wanted the answers too, but her response shocked me.

'Raped women are already damaged goods, so why damage them further with an abortion?'

My heart was pounding. While I'd prepared as much as I could for the content of the show, this really threw me. Straightening myself up, I bit at the scar tissue inside my mouth while the doctor marched on past me, holding up her banner and singing. I didn't tell her I'd been raped but as I was shunted from side to side by pro-lifers banging their drums in the crowd, I felt a surge of anger. I am not 'damaged goods' and neither is an eleven-year-old girl. No one who's been raped should be called 'damaged goods'.

Next I met a woman named Cathy. She was also marching and singing, but a few minutes into our chat she confessed that she had run abortion clinics in the past and now felt extreme remorse for her actions and wanted all such clinics banned. I asked her whether she realised that, if abortion became illegal in one state, women would simply drive a couple of hours over the border to a state where it was legal.

'I don't know about that but I know it has to be made illegal in this state,' she replied.

To my horror, there were also children on the march, holding signs saying 'Baby Killers Must Die' and 'Stop Stem-Cell Research Now!' Half of them were too young even to read; they were clearly just being used for shock value by adults with an agenda to push. It was terrifying to think how ill informed and narrow minded those kids will likely be as they grow up, being taught just one side of the argument. I couldn't help but feel these views really had nothing to do with religion and that the protesters were all caught up in a fearful, mindless, ill-educated fervour.

After the rally we went back to the church where I was given the opportunity to explain the procedure I was hoping to have. Despite the fact I told them I wasn't getting stem cells from an embryo, and that mine were coming from a deceased, consenting adult donor, the topic moved from my operation to the subject of me and my morals. The protestors said I was selfish and shouldn't be allowed to have the treatment. One woman was vehement and irrational in her opposition and attacked me verbally. 'You've been touched by Satan. You're being punished for what you did in a past life. You should learn to live with it.'

I was seething but tried to keep a cool head. I was not there to have a smack down in a house of God.

It didn't matter how many times I tried to explain my belief in the stem-cell treatment, they all thought I was immoral, and that I should accept that losing my sight was somehow my own fault. When I tried to suggest that their protesting was putting a stop to valuable research that could save them or a family member from cancer or heart disease, they claimed ignorance and said they didn't want to know anything about it. They seemed to revel in being completely closed-minded. I was happy when it was time to leave them behind and head back to the airport for our flight home; it had been a manic few days of filming. The minute I got back into my flat I hung Dr Taylor's postcard on my wall where I could clearly see it.

The following week, I was in hospital being prepped for my stem-cell eye surgery with Mr Daya. I counted up all the surgeries I'd been through since the attack, and worked out that this was to be my 110th. It lasted an hour – peanuts compared with some I've had, but the hard part was the week-long wait afterwards to see how successful it had been, quite literally. It seemed to drag on forever.

Finally the day arrived to remove the bandages and take out the stitches. Mr Daya was as excited as I was. He prepared me for what to expect.

'Your eye will take a while to focus, so just keep calm and give yourself a few minutes, okay?'

I nodded and slowly opened my eye, blinking several times. I felt a rush of adrenaline.

'I can see!'

'Okay, Katie. Tell me what you can see.'

I held my hand up to my face, it was fuzzy but I could make out all my fingers and could see the pink nail polish I had on. I started laughing, turning to look at Mr Daya. It was like a miracle.

'I can see you and I can see my hand.'

I looked out the window.

'I can see out the window.'

I looked at his desk.

'I can see your desk.'

At the door.

'I can see the door!'

It had worked.

Everything was blurred and grainy but it felt like the world had just doubled in size. My sight wasn't back to where it had been before the attack, but gaining at least some vision in my bad eye, and therefore some depth perception, left me feeling dizzy and giddy with excitement.

I spent hours when I got home just looking at everything, checking my reflection from all angles, everything I hadn't been able to see properly since the attack. One more part of the Katie Piper that my attackers had tried to destroy was restored. I was taking ownership of my life, moving on, moving forward. I was filled with joy, hope and positivity.

Chapter Twelve

My new vision was a cause for celebration, so I planned a lunch with Kay the following weekend. Plus, I hadn't seen her since I'd returned from filming and we had lots to catch up on.

We met at one of our favourite haunts and she gave me her trademark tight hug and held me by the shoulders as she peered into my left eye.

'You look fantastic, Tiny, how does it feel?'

'Amazing. It's taking me half the time to do my hair now.'

'Ha, you can tell.'

'Thanks!'

We laughed and were led to our table where we ordered drinks and settled down for a proper chat.

'I can't believe I haven't seen you since you got back from America. How was it?'

'Oh my God, it was amazing. Forgive the pun but it was an eye-opener in more ways than one.'

'Kate, that's a bad joke.'

'No seriously, it really was. Some of the people I met were incredibly inspirational and others were quite scary. Promise me, if you ever become a mum you won't turn your kid into a nutter.'

I took a sip of my drink but could see her looking furtively down at the floor, avoiding my stare.

'Hmm . . . yep. I promise.'

'Kay?'

'Yeah.'

'What aren't you telling me?'

I pulled back, giving her the best quizzical look I could.

'Nothing, no, nothing. What else happened? What were the film crew like?'

I knew she was avoiding telling me something.

'Kay, I'm serious. I know you better than you know yourself. What's on your mind?'

She looked up at me.

'I've . . . We've . . . Well it's funny you said what you just did because Ivan and I have been thinking about having a baby.'

'*What*?!'

I knew they were engaged but had presumed they were planning to tie the knot before starting a family. She couldn't have surprised me any more if she'd tried.

'We can't afford a wedding at the moment and have talked long and hard about what we want so we've decided to do things the other way round and have a baby first.'

'Oh . . . My . . . God!'

She laughed.

'Hang on, I'm not pregnant yet! You're my best friend and I wanted to share it with you. We'll start trying in the next few months. It might not happen at all but I wanted to know what you thought.'

I reached over the table and squeezed her hand.

'Oh Kay. I'm so happy for you, really I am. I hope it happens for you, you know how much I want you to be happy. I wasn't expecting this is all. I've sort of ruled out that it could happen for me so I guess in a weird way I'd not really considered it would happen just yet for my mates. But you're going to be a completely amazing mum and I'm going to be a completely amazing Aunty Kate.'

We chatted about names and timescales over lunch, but as we paid up, I couldn't help but look around the restaurant, watching couples at other tables. I don't know why Kay's news was such a surprise to me. We were in our late twenties, when lots of people settle down and start thinking about kids.

I woke up the next morning feeling strangely insecure. If Kay turned out to be just the first of many friends to get pregnant, I'd soon be sitting in on my own again, not through choice but because everyone else would be busy with their new families, changing nappies while I changed TV channels. It got me thinking. When I first moved into my little Chiswick flat I wasn't sure what my future would hold exactly, but somewhere deep down I'd dared to dream that it would include finding love, happiness, a man, and hopefully having a family. But with no man on the horizon and the potential risk of infertility from the anti-rejection drugs I was on after my eye operation, as well as more generally, as a result of all my operations and trauma, there was a distinct chance I couldn't have a baby myself even if I wanted to. My usual Kate-Can-Fix-It mentality suddenly kicked in and I went into action mode, looking into non-traditional routes to motherhood. I soon became curious about adoption.

The more I thought about it, the more it appealed to me. Mine might not be as conventional a family as the one I grew up in, but maybe I could have my own little unit nonetheless. After listing the pros and cons, it seemed like it could be the perfect solution.

In the New Year I met up with a broody Kay for lunch and told her my plans. She was surprised but when I reasoned it all out with her she told me she'd do everything she could to support me. I swore her to secrecy and spent the next few months researching different adoption agencies in the UK. I figured it would likely be a very long and arduous process to adopt as a single woman who was also disabled and disfigured. I wondered if the counselling and therapy, and the fact I'd suffered from post-traumatic stress disorder (PTSD) after the attack, would be seen as a history of mental health issues, which could prolong the process even more.

Undeterred, I suddenly had a thought. Anyone who knows me knows how inspired I am by the surgeon who saved my life, Mr Jawad. He devotes considerable volunteer time and surgical skills to help acid victims in Pakistan, where he is from. I remembered him telling me once about the many children he knew or had operated on that were burned by acid as a consequence of being near or in the arms of their mothers when the women were attacked by their husbands. Little children, whose mums had died as a result of their injuries, were forced into orphanages and treated like freaks. I felt that as a woman who had been attacked in such a way, I'd understand the complexities of their emotions and the medical care such a child needs, and that I could help give a little person like this a chance in life. The more I thought about it, the more determined I became.

I told Kay about my plans on the phone.

At the Pride of Britain ceremony, holding my special recognition award. It was the first time I won something for my work with the charity, and was a huge step forward for me.

On the red carpet for Pride of Britain with Mr Jawad, the surgeon who gave me back my life.

Pride of Britain, one year on: this time as a judge, not a nominee! The judging panel included some amazing people – I was so flattered to be picked alongside them.

At the Katie Piper Foundation's charity ball with Jahméne Douglas, who performed that night. Jahméne's mother suffered burns when abused by his father, so he's a great supporter of the charity, as well as a great friend of mine.

With one of my favourite guests on my new series *Bodyshockers*.

In Tanzania visiting a local orphanage whilst working on a charity trip with the Northern Burn Care unit.

In the make-up room before some filming, this time in Poland. Expanding my TV work has taken me all over the world and helped me meet extraordinary people.

Just about to carry the Paralympic torch: it was a huge privilege, and I was more nervous than I look…

…and afterwards, back home with my very own torch (they let you keep it!).

A bike ride with my gorgeous sister Suzy.

Training for my half-marathon. I might not look very cheerful, but running gave me something positive to aim for and helped me get back on an even keel.

After the Royal Parks Half Marathon, feeling very proud of myself!

'The chances are none of these kids will be adopted, because they look like me and so nobody wants them. But I can make a difference to them and they can make a difference to me.'

She was so supportive.

'Oh my God, Kate, that would be incredible. You're sure that's what you want?'

I was emphatic.

'I'm saving money already. I'm not going to do anything rash though. I'll take my time looking into it properly and then when I'm ready I'll start the process. It could take years for me to be approved but it's what I want so I'll wait as long as it takes.'

My heart swelled every time I thought about it. I decided I'd wait until I was a bit further down the path before telling Mum and Dad. I knew they'd say I hadn't thought it through and I didn't want to have to start defending myself until I knew timescales and more about what the process entailed.

With my plan in place, and work going well, I started spending more time with my family and friends. I was finally feeling comfortable with being single, figuring that at least I didn't have to check plans with anyone and could do what I wanted when I wanted. So with that in mind, and with Suzy's birthday in just a couple of weeks, it seemed like the perfect opportunity to organise a last-minute girls' trip to New York for just the two of us. We hadn't been away together since Amsterdam, and while she was still enjoying teasing me about our sex-show encounter, I wanted to surprise her and show her how much she meant to me.

Chapter Thirteen

At my next Sunday lunch at Mum and Dad's, Suzy and I spent most of the time together finalising the plans I'd been putting into action for our trip, but I also made sure that I had quality time with my parents too. Now that my visits home were less frequent than they used to be before work had taken over, these occasions had become even more special.

My family were always pleased to see me, but it was our dog Barclay who usually made the biggest fuss when I'd visit. I'd barely get through the door before he'd come charging towards me, desperate to be scooped up and cuddled. He'd race around the living room bringing me his toys until I relented and sat on the sofa so he could snuggle up next to me for a nap. This Sunday was no different, and I made sure that Barclay got just as much attention as everyone else.

That day we went through the usual Sunday routine, and after a full-on lunch and we'd all caught up with each other's latest news, I said my goodbyes to Mum and Dad and gave Barclay one final cuddle before I headed back to London for another busy week ahead.

As I opened the door to my flat I heard the phone start to ring. It was Dad. I was sure he was calling to tell me I'd left something behind.

'Hi Dad.'

'Kate, love, it's Barclay . . .'

His voice trailed off.

'Dad, what is it? Has he run away?'

He'd never gone missing before but I wondered whether he'd tried to chase my car up the road. He always hated it when I left.

Dad explained that after I'd left to go home Barclay had had a coughing fit and they'd found him in the kitchen under the table, limp and lifeless. They'd rushed him to the vet across the road but he'd had a heart attack and was brain damaged, and the vet said he would never recover and that it would be kindest to put him out of his misery. My throat tightened. My Barclay couldn't be gone . . .

'But Dad, I just saw him, he was fine! I don't understand . . .'

'Kate, he wasn't a young dog anymore. We all loved him but at least he didn't suffer.'

Dad was as heartbroken as I was and he kept pausing to compose himself as he explained that the vet would have him cremated and we'd get his ashes in a few days' time. As I hung up the phone, tears streamed from my eyes. I felt bereft.

Barclay had been my canine rock during my recovery and was a huge part of my support team. When I was discharged from hospital, I was sure he wouldn't recognise me: my old face was gone – red raw and unrecognisable behind a plastic mask. My head was shaved and I presumed he'd be terrified of me. But the minute I got back home he'd leaped at me like I'd never been away and as if I didn't look different.

During the months on end when I stayed in watching comedy box sets, he'd sit protectively by my side. When I was filming my first documentary, one of the all-female crew called in sick and they sent a male sound technician in her place. Barclay knew instantly I was nervous. When they tried to shut him away to film an interview with me, he barked, yelped and scratched until they relented – he sat vigilantly on my lap during the entire interview.

At the end of *My Beautiful Face*, I'm shown walking to the shops with my ever-faithful, loyal and loving companion by my side. Barclay stayed by me as I cried tears of frustration during my recovery, gently licking them off my hand as they fell from my plastic mask. He was there for me when I was suffering and after I got the news from Dad I couldn't help but feel I hadn't been able to help him, comfort him or reassure him when it was his turn. Lying in bed that night, I cried tears of grief for hours. My friend who'd helped put me back together was gone forever.

Going back to Mum and Dad's on the day Barclay was cremated was so hard. The house seemed empty and quiet without him racing round and squeaking his toys. Sitting on the sofa after lunch, I kept putting my hand down by my side to where he usually sat, expecting to feel his warm fluffy coat, then remembering with a hurting heart that he was gone.

My parents let me have his ashes and I put them in a little urn beside my bed. I spent the next two days finding old photographs of him and planned to make a montage of memories to put on my wall as soon as I got back from New York.

Although we were both really upset by Barclay's death, Suzy and I decided to go ahead with our trip, reasoning that it would help take our minds off how much we missed him. Besides, *Things*

Get Better was due out very soon and I wanted to spend some quality time with my little sister before the rounds of book publicity kicked in.

The weekend before we left, I went over to my friend Juliet's house in Essex to borrow a suitcase. Her boyfriend Mark answered the door.

'Hey, Kate, I'm on my way out, Juliet's upstairs. Have a fab time in New York.'

'Thanks, Mark, see you later.'

I smiled and jogged upstairs. Juliet gave me a big hug and asked how I was feeling. I assured her I was fine and followed her to put the kettle on as she lugged out the case for me. I could sense she was itching to tell me something. She blurted it out before the kettle had even boiled.

'Mark's mate James fancies you.'

I stopped dead. I wasn't sure I'd heard her right. No one had said anything remotely like this since the attack, and somewhere deep down it awakened a sense-memory of my old life.

'What do you *mean* he fancies me? He's never met me, how does he even know me?'

'Duh, he saw a photo of you and me together. He asked Mark to ask me to ask you if he can have your number. He said he wants to meet you.'

'Uh-uh. No. No way. Never.' I waved my hands around in protest.

'Kate, don't be so negative. You never know, he could be "the one".' She gave me an encouraging look.

'Nope, he won't be. No. Seriously, Juliet, I'm not meeting him.'

'Why?'

I put my hands on my hips and took a deep breath.

'I know the picture you're talking about. A) That picture is tiny, B) it was taken at arm's length, C) it was taken in the dark when I was totally made up and my hair was perfect. It's about a gazillion bajillion miles away from how I actually look. You know you can't see my burns in that photo. He'll meet me and be really gutted and do a runner. I have no desire to put myself through watching yet another person's face drop when they see me in real life. He'll be disappointed. I know he will.'

Juliet put her hands on my shoulders, her voice soft and low.

'Kate, you don't know him. You don't know what he'll think of you. Why don't you give him a chance? Mark says he's a really stand-up, nice, decent guy.'

I still wasn't convinced.

'Okay, trust me on this, these will be the first four thoughts that come into his head: "God she looks weird, I wonder what happened to her face?" Then he'll get closer and think "Eurgh, that girl looks a right state, she's had way too much plastic surgery and Botox." He may then recognise me and then he'll think, "Oh, she's that acid girl, poor thing." Then maybe finally, "She's an inspiration to my mum/sister/female friend (delete as appropriate) maybe I should get a photo/autograph for them." '

Juliet was laughing and even I couldn't help but smile. But I knew she got the point I was trying to make. I'd worked hard to protect myself emotionally since my bad run of dating. Yes, I still longed for companionship but the last thing I wanted to do was put my heart on a plate just so someone could trample on it all over again.

'I'm serious, Juliet. You know what I've been through in the last twelve months. I can't take another knock. Besides, I'm totally busy with work. Even if he was perfect and really into me, I've got far too much on my plate for a relationship at the moment.'

It was an excuse but I was emphatic. I'd spent years protecting my skin and my scars and now I'd realised it was time to start being more protective of my heart too.

I was adamant, but so was Juliet.

'Kate, listen. If you don't try, you may be missing out on an opportunity. I know what you've been through but you can't lock yourself away forever. At some point you're going to have to give some bloke the benefit of the doubt. Isn't it better that it's a friend of a friend rather than a complete stranger in a pub?'

While I hated to admit it, her argument had merit. I'd stopped trying to find a man but I still wanted to be wanted. Sometimes I craved a good, old-fashioned, pulse-quickening flirt, that first flush of excitement when you get a text message or that light-headed dizziness when you share a kiss, that electric charge when you hold one another's gaze.

Juliet could see my resolve beginning to weaken. I started to question her.

'Does he know I'm *that* girl? Did Mark tell him I'm disfigured? I don't want him to meet me out of fascination and I don't want him to meet me if he doesn't know I'm burned.'

'I think he knows who you are, he knows your name . . . Mark asked me to ask you last week but I didn't think you were ready, especially as you were upset about Barclay. James is really keen, Kate. He's really family-orientated like you and he cares about what's on the inside of a person. He's a great catch, I promise. Cross my heart. Oh, and he's really fit.'

She handed me her phone to show me a tiny pixellated photo of him.

'See, he is, isn't he?'

'Juliet, I can just about make out that this is a bloke with hair, two eyes, a nose and a mouth. I can barely see him here, so how will I even know it's him if . . . I repeat . . . IF we meet?'

'Sorry! I promise you'll adore him though.'

She squeezed my hand and a smile broke out across my face. By this time my curiosity was killing me and I finally relented.

'Okay, give him my number and we'll see where things go from there, but I'm warning you, Juliet, if he turns out to be a loser I'm never going near a man again.'

I didn't have much chance to think about James over the next few days before Suzy and I left for New York; I was busy holding a workshop in London and doing voiceover work for my programmes for Channel 4, not to mention psyching myself up for my first-ever book signing (I'd succumbed this time around, having not felt strong or brave enough to do these when *Beautiful* had been published). Besides, I was sure it would all go wrong with James so I tried to put it out of my head, believing there wasn't much point in getting excited.

The day before Suzy and I left, just as I was getting ready for an early night, my phone beeped into life with a message from a number I didn't recognise.

'Hi Katie, it's James. I got your number from Mark. How are you? xx'

I got butterflies.

'Hi James, I'm good thanks, how are you?'

'Good. Thanks for letting me have your number. How's your day been?'

In actual fact I'd been at a meeting at my publishers that day, finalising the details of the book signing, but I thought it might sound too grand to tell him that in our first texts, so I decided to keep my reply simple.

'Great, busy. I'm taking my sister away for her birthday tomorrow so trying to get everything done.'

'Have a great time, maybe we can get together for a drink when you get back? If you'd like to?'

Just the thought of a date with a new man made me feel nauseated, but also very excited.

'I'll text you when I'm back.'

'Great, have fun xxx'

Chapter Fourteen

The New York trip was supposed to be all about Suzy but I was so flustered I spent the entire time in Manhattan bending her ear about James and debating out loud whether I should actually go out with him or not. I leaned on her for advice, sounding like a scared, naive teenager about to start dating for the very first time.

'Juliet knows what you've been through,' she counselled. 'She wouldn't fix you up with just anyone. If she says he's nice then you should give him a chance. Besides, it's just a drink, Kate. It's not like he's asking you to spend the rest of your life with him.'

After a successful (and expensive!) trip, I'd barely got home when my phone buzzed in my jacket pocket.

'Hi Kate, it's James. Are you back yet? Did you have a good time? xx'

I let myself in, shut the door and fumbled with my phone. I'd half expected him to have forgotten me while I was away.

'Yep, spent far too much money but it was great. How are you?'

'Busy at work for the next few weeks but are you free at the end of the month?'

I hesitated: this was the crunch moment. I realised I had to give him an answer. The best I could manage was:

'Not sure. Think so.'

But that was enough to keep us going.

Over the next fortnight we started texting every day. He always asked if I'd had a good day and what I'd been up to. He seemed genuinely interested in me and I could feel myself getting hopeful.

Soon we upgraded to phoning, rather than texting. I generally feel very comfortable talking on the phone because there's no judgement about appearance, but even so, our first phone call was a little nervous and stilted, not least because I could hardly understand a word he said. Juliet had neglected to tell me he was an Eastender with a strong Cockney accent! While I was getting familiar with his voice, I'd have to make sure everything around me was totally silent so I could concentrate completely on what he was saying. If I were driving, I'd ignore his call on my hands free and phone him back the second I got inside. (It's a miracle I didn't get a speeding ticket.) On one occasion he surprised me by ringing half an hour earlier than we'd agreed. My washing machine was on and it may as well have been Apollo Eleven taking off. I frantically tried to turn it off, pressing every button in desperation while the phone rang in my hand. Giving up, I darted into the bedroom, climbed into my wardrobe and closed the doors so I could hear him properly . . . That's how excited I was to speak to him!

Soon we were talking easily: flirting, joking and teasing, with all the safety that comes with not actually being face to face. I told him I worked for a charity, and was ready to tell him which one if he asked, but he didn't. He told me he was a carpenter. We talked about family and friends, including Mark and Juliet, and how they'd schemed to set us up.

I'd sit in bed and we'd 'hang out' on the phone, watching the same TV show and talking about whether it was any good or not. One evening there was a pause in our usually fluid conversation.

'So, Kate, I'm free next Friday if you are. I thought we could maybe have a drink and go to the cinema if you fancy it?'

The adrenaline rush was overwhelming and I panicked.

'Oh, ah, I don't know. Can I let you know tomorrow?'

'Sure, I'll call you after work, okay? Good night.'

'Night.'

I hung up and immediately got out of bed and started pacing around my flat. Things were going so well between us so far. He was making me laugh and I liked him, but I was still sure it was all going to go wrong when he met me. I spent a sleepless night wondering why things couldn't just stay the way they were.

The next day I was supposed to be focusing on work, but it was hard not to be distracted. I had a crazy schedule packed with fifteen press and radio interviews for the book, and I talked for hours about coping mechanisms, finding strength, seeing the bright side and believing in yourself, about gaining confidence, holding your head high . . . But despite what should effectively have been a ten-hour pep talk with myself about how to cope with that night's pending conversation with James, I was still a jangling bag of nerves. It didn't help that when I finally got home, the phone call that had been on my mind all day long was only an hour away.

I made a fast dinner and had just finished my last mouthful of pasta when my phone started ringing. It was him. I let it ring just long enough before finally picking it up.

'Hi Kate, how was your day?'

I kept quiet about the fact that I'd thought of nothing but him and this moment for nearly twenty-four hours.

'Yeah, busy. You?' I was trying hard to sound casual.

'Same. Started at seven this morning and I've only just finished. I'm on my way home now. Did you have a think about next weekend? Are you free Friday?'

I took a deep breath.

'Yeah I did, I am. I mean, yes. If you're still free. If you're not, don't worry though . . .'

I cringed at how lame and nervous I sounded, wanting to reel the words back into my mouth.

'No, that'd be great. You're in West London right? I'll come to you. I'll call you tomorrow and we can finalise the details, that okay?'

'Yeah, sure. Have a good night.'

'Thanks, Kate. I'm really looking forward to Friday. See you later.'

The minute I hung up I started replaying and analysing the whole conversation in my head, like some paranoid forensic detective trying to anticipate out his motives. 'Why does he want to come all the way here from the East End? He could find out where I live and kill me. But then it's better if he comes to me because then I'm closer to home if he does try to kill me; I might be able to make it back home to safety. But then he'll know where to come back and find me . . .' I knew my thoughts were irrational; Juliet's boyfriend knew James really well and had vetted him, but the worries kept racing through my mind nonetheless. I knew I was overreacting and that I wasn't trusting my judgement. I hadn't seen any signs saying he was anything other than a really nice guy. I weighed up the mental pros and cons and decided it was indeed better if he came to me. Besides, he probably wouldn't even get the chance to kill me because I was sure he'd cancel before he even got here.

After a few fretful days, the day of the date finally arrived. As I got out of the shower I realised I hated first dates more than I hated hospital appointments or even skin grafts. I felt queasy thinking about the initial small talk:

'So where did you grow up? Where exactly do you live? Got any hobbies?'

Even though James and I had already covered an awful lot of ground over the phone, I hadn't yet told him in detail about my work or my personal life. How was that going to play out?

'You know I said I work for a charity? Well it's mine and I set it up. It's a burns charity because I'm burned. Oh, and I make programmes for Channel 4 because they did a documentary about me being raped and having acid thrown in my face. And I don't want to tell you where I live because I'm paranoid about safety in case you or the guys who did it to me come back and try to kill me. Next weekend? Yeah, I'm doing a book signing for my second book then having an operation on my throat to get rid of some scar tissue from when I swallowed the acid.'

This was all intensely private, delicate stuff that I didn't like saying out loud to anyone, let alone anything I felt comfortable chatting about over a drink with someone I barely knew. But there was no way of avoiding it.

We'd planned to get together at seven o'clock for a drink in a local bar and then go on to the cinema. I'd wanted to do something different, but I didn't want to be the one to suggest anything. I didn't like the thought of talking for just twenty minutes or so, then sitting in the dark for an hour and a half, mere inches from one another. Although, I figured that if he did turn out to be a starer, at least going to the cinema would keep his eyes busy elsewhere than on my scars.

I started doing my make-up, but as the clock ticked past 5:30, it still felt a bit unreal and like the evening wasn't going to happen. There was plenty of time for James to come to his senses and call the whole thing off.

Forty-five minutes later, my bedroom looked like a bomb had gone off at Topshop. All the clothes I'd bought in New York were in a pile on the floor and I was no nearer to deciding what the hell to wear. With my trackies still on, I started talking out loud into my wardrobe. 'I don't want to wear anything too provocative, but I also don't want to look like a Sunday school teacher. Should I go for something that shows the scars on my neck or something buttoned up that will keep them hidden? If I show them, at least there won't be a big "reveal" a few dates down the line . . . if we ever get that far.'

My friends and family were all great for advice, but at times like this I felt alone in my decision-making because none of them had been through what I had. I didn't feel I could ask anyone whether or not to show my scarred cleavage – because no one else *had* a scarred cleavage. While they were all empathetic, none of them could completely relate to my point-blank refusal to meet in a lobby or outside, or anywhere with bright lights. The list of doubts, fears and anxieties I felt I had to deal with on my own were endless and exhausting. My hopes, along with all my clothes, were on the floor.

After three outfit changes, I figured I was looking the best I possibly could. I chose a long, loose red checked shirt, black pleather leggings, black stilettos and a black handbag. I checked myself out in the mirror. The outfit wasn't perfect but it trod the right side of 'yeah-I'm-burned-it's-not-a-big-deal-for-me-is-it-a-big-deal-for-you?'

I checked my watch at ten minutes to seven. I could drive to the bar in about five minutes. I was just putting my lipstick in my handbag when the phone rang. With a sinking heart, I prepared myself for the worst. James said: 'I'm really sorry, Kate, I'm stuck in awful traffic and I'm probably going to be at least forty minutes late. I didn't get out of work as early as I thought I would.'

I attempted to sound nonchalant, 'No problem. I'm running hideously late too. I was just about to call . . .'

We adjusted our timings and after hanging up I turned back to the mirror, clearing my throat and trying to hold my head up. I was sure he was lying and that he wasn't coming at all. I was devastated. I sunk onto the sofa and prepared myself for yet another night in front of the TV. But forty minutes later, as promised, the phone rang.

'Are you here? I'm parking up. Shall I find you and we can walk in together?'

I couldn't believe it. I started fumbling with my coat with one hand while still clutching the phone with the other.

'I'm . . . .'

I dropped my car keys on the floor and nearly launched the phone out of my hand as I rammed my feet into my shoes. Grabbing at my keys, I recovered myself.

'I'm still running late, I'll be there in ten minutes.'

Thank God I hadn't bothered to take off my make-up and change into my PJs! I dashed out to the car. With traffic on my side, I could really make it in four minutes and not keep him waiting too long.

Sod's law, traffic wasn't on my side. My heart was pounding as I sat at red light after red light. My mind was racing all over the place. What if he'd grown sick of waiting and had gone? What if he was standing waiting for me and I'd have to walk up to him? I didn't want him to see me walk. What if I fell over?

I finally pulled into the car park. My hands were sweating and I felt like my make-up was starting to slip. I wanted to go to the loo first so I could make sure I looked presentable, but a text from him told me he was already in the bar. Scuppered.

I walked in, searching desperately for the face that matched the photo Juliet had shown me on her phone. I couldn't see anyone fitting his description. There was a guy sitting at the end of the bar who I thought kind of matched the picture but he looked about fifty, not the twenty-eight I knew James was. Scrabbling in my bag for my mobile, I called his number and thankfully the guy at the bar didn't reach for his phone.

'I can't see you, are you in here?'

'I just went to the toilet, I'm coming out now.'

The toilet door opened and out walked a tall dark stranger on his phone. My head felt light but through the dizziness I could see he was absolutely gorgeous. I couldn't believe this was finally happening. We caught one another's eye, each smiled and hung up. I didn't want to hug or kiss him in case he got freaked out by touching me, so I did a kind of lame half-wave as he approached. He hugged me anyway and we sat down.

'I'm so sorry for being late, Kate, I hope you're not too angry with me.'

'God no, I was later than you, remember? I'm sorry too.'

'You look nice.'

I looked up at him, wondering if he really meant it.

'Oh, thanks, you do too. How was work today?'

There was lots of nervous, excited rambling on both our parts. I talked too much, half terrified of continually saying 'pardon', what with the background music and busy chatter of the bar. I was concentrating so hard on listening to him that I soon forgot my nerves, and ten minutes in we were both joking and laughing. So far, so different from my usual dates. I was used to stilted silences and awkward stares. James was chatty, witty and looked me squarely in the eye. It seemed things were going well, but I didn't want to get my hopes up. When it came to reading signals from blokes, I may as well have been totally blind. I'd lost confidence in my ability to judge things properly.

I'm sure we could have kept talking for hours but we finished our drinks and made our way into the cinema to see a later showing of the film than we'd originally planned. Sitting next to each other in silence felt a little strange but it gave me a good chance to steal sideways glances at him and check out his body language. I liked how he threw his head back when he laughed, the way his nose twitched a bit when he smiled. The fact he threw popcorn into his mouth rather than put it in and how he shifted in his seat continually trying to find a comfy spot. I noticed we both laughed at the same bits of the film, which felt like a good sign.

Afterwards, we decided to go for a coffee. I started to actually believe the date was going quite well. He asked me if I had a busy week coming up. Juliet had told him about the Foundation before we met and he was interested to learn more.

'So, how does it work day to day at your charity? What kind of things are you doing?'

I felt comfortable now telling him more.

'We do lots of things, like organise social events and classes which bring people with burns and scars together. It's rewarding, and fun. We provide different treatments and advice about camouflage make-up. There's the admin side of it too, we get hundreds of letters every week from people coping with all kinds of disfigurement and we organise charity balls and fundraising events. All kinds of stuff like that.'

'Oh, okay. Bet that's busy.'

'Yeah it is, but I love it.'

That was it. He hadn't made a big deal out of it at all, he just took it at face value and thankfully didn't ask any more questions about it just then. Then he told me more about his job as a carpenter and the sites he worked on. We exchanged stories about our respective families, and discussed the differences between East and West London – including the accent! It was all so normal, and it felt fantastic.

He never once mentioned my burns, and because he didn't, I didn't either. He didn't even stare at them, and so I didn't feel self-conscious. Being looked in the eye rather than being stared at had me relaxed and buzzing with confidence.

It was gone midnight by the time we decided to each head home. He walked me to my car and I offered to drive him back to his. When we reached his car, he turned to face me as we sat there.

'Thanks, Kate, I had a really great night.'

'Yeah, me too. Good movie.'

'Good company too.'

I was sure he could hear my heart pounding in my chest. I'd had the best night in years, and I had a feeling he'd had a good night too. If my girly intuition was right, this was the moment when we'd kiss . . .

He leaned in but I had only been half-right. He went for a gentlemanly peck on the cheek but I was swept up in the moment and went straight in, open-mouthed, for a full-on kiss. There was no hiding it, and what we ended up with was a cringingly awkward, moist half-kiss, my mouth landing on his cheek at the last minute. I might as well have licked him! The searing, sweaty, hot and embarrassed feelings I'd had on the way to our date resurfaced tenfold. I instantly hated myself.

He reached for the car door.

'I'll give you a call.'

'Okay, erm, bye James.'

I drove off the second the door closed, cringing with embarrassment at what a dating amateur I was. I imagined him driving out the car park thinking 'what a weirdo, why did she lick me?'

I rang my friend Samuel straight away.

'You won't believe what I just did. A-w-k-w-a-r-d . . .' I told him the whole cringeworthy scene, then added. 'Well, I'm sure I'm never going to see him again. I wouldn't blame him if he thought I was some kind of tongue fetishist.'

He erupted in laughter before reassuring me. 'Kate, it just couldn't have been that bad. You're probably totally overreacting. It really does sound funny rather than horrific. I'm sure he thought it was . . . uh . . . charming.'

We laughed again and hung up, but I half-wondered if I really had messed it up.

Suzy called on Saturday morning to see how it went.

'Well?'

I tried to sound casual.

'Yeah it was okay, I don't think I'll see him again though.'

'Why not, if it went okay?'

'I don't know, just a feeling. Hey, you fancy coming to stay next weekend?'

Suzy accepted my offer but took the hint and didn't pursue the subject. I was supposed to be going to Mum and Dad's for Sunday lunch the next day but I cancelled, using work as an excuse, and spent the day at the charity. If I was moping I may as well try to be productive over at the Foundation and distract myself from my idiocy somehow. But as I sat alone eating chocolate for lunch from the office vending machine, and got on top of a huge pile of correspondence, I still couldn't completely keep myself from wondering whether I'd ever hear from James again.

Chapter Fifteen

Thankfully the Foundation continued to provide the distraction from my love life that I needed. We'd been working on a big two-day educational event called Scar Academy UK, with Oscare (a Belgian organization) and Queen Mary University. Which was aimed at professionals working in the area of scar management. It would offer talks, lectures and demonstrations and we were hoping to give a bursary to every burns unit in the country to send a representative to participate. This was set to be one of the biggest events we had hosted, and it needed a lot of my time and attention, so I had plenty to occupy me and keep my mind off my date with James – and how it ended! Every time I felt the memory of that hideous kiss come bubbling to the surface, I was able to push it back down and focus on the next task in front of me rather than dwell on the embarrassment I felt about that night.

The publication of *Things Get Better* was also about to give me another much-needed pick-me-up, especially with my book signing coming up. It had been arranged to take place in the book department of Selfridges. I had reluctantly agreed to it, but I was still half-petrified I'd be attacked since it had been made so public and was widely advertised – which is one reason I didn't do a signing for my first book – and also half-terrified that no one would actually turn up. On the day I was a nervous wreck, and when I arrived I made a mental note of where the exits were and planned what I would do if anyone came at me. I knew deep down the chances that anyone would want to hurt me were very slim, but when you've experienced the kind of senseless violence that I have, it's not always easy to keep thinking rational, particularly in times of high stress. I practised all my relaxation techniques, and although I tried to smile and be cheerful while I sat with friends and colleagues in a side room as the signing spot on the shop floor was being prepared, I still felt incredibly tense.

I turned my attention momentarily to my Twitter page to browse through some of the results of a campaign we'd started as part of the celebrations for the book, called Katie's Army. Its mission was to spread positivity and healing, and I had been asking people to share their random acts of kindness. Although early days, the response had already been overwhelming. One man tweeted me saying he'd left his change in the vending machine at college so the next person who came along could get a chocolate bar on him. A woman told me she'd bought her son a Happy Meal after he helped another boy at school pick up the contents of his bag that had spilled out on the floor. Someone tweeted that she'd made a special dinner for her brother after finding out he'd helped an old man who'd fallen over in the street. Another man bought a bunch of flowers for an elderly neighbour after hearing that her husband had passed away.

Feeling inspired by all their acts of goodwill, and knowing I was supported by people I hadn't even met, I drew back my shoulders, took a deep breath and prepared to enter the room where the signing would happen. As I did so I could see there was already a long queue of both women and men who were waiting to talk to me and have me sign their books. At the sight of all their friendly faces my racing heart slowed and I started to relax and allow myself to completely enjoy the moment.

Many of the people who had taken the time to come along had been writing me letters, emails and tweets of support for years. I met so many great people, who I already felt I knew so much about, in person for the first time. Meeting them face-to-face was fantastic; it was a real delight to finally be able to put faces and smiles to profiles or Twitter handles. They'd come from Manchester, Liverpool, Bristol, all over the UK. A lot of them had scars too, some physical, some emotional, and some both, that they were trying to come to terms with. Meeting them and hearing their stories and words of encouragement left me feeling incredibly humbled. It also made me feel like the book really *could* help and live up to its title, which is what I dreamed of.

By the end of the day I was on such a high and Katie's Army was trending on Twitter. The campaign wasn't about gratitude or reward, it was about knowing you'd done something, no matter how small, to make someone else's day that little bit brighter, and made them believe that things could get better. And every single person who came to the book signing had done just that for me.

It had been an incredible day, but that wasn't the end of it. As I drove home my phone beeped beside me.

'Hi Kate, how are you? I had a great time on Friday. What are your plans for the weekend? James xx'

I had just about consigned James to the history books and written off the date as yet more proof I'd be single forever, so his text took me completely by surprise. Once again I couldn't help trying to analyse his words, and spent half an hour reading and re-reading his message.

'*Your plans.*' What did he mean? Was he asking if I was free that weekend so we could spend some time together? Or was he hoping I was already busy so he didn't have to make any excuses? Should I pretend to be busy so I seemed popular and interesting and he'd be spared having to tell me he wasn't free? Was it a trick? Was he just being polite?

I drafted and deleted at least seventeen texts back to him before I plucked up the courage to finally write something and press send.

'Thanks, I had a good time too. Not sure what I'm doing this weekend, what about you?'

My phone was quiet for a few minutes. I figured the worst, as usual. But what came back was this:

'Fancy meeting up in Shoreditch? It's kind of halfway. We could go for drinks then have dinner?'

A huge grin spread over my face and I felt the most incredible relief. He *did* want to see me again. He even wanted to take me out. This time on a proper date, not just to the cinema. I knew by then that I fancied him, and it seemed like maybe – just maybe – I hadn't completely ruined things. I texted back and we arranged to meet at the Hoxton Grill. With a chink of light beaming in my personal life, and with the success of the signing still fresh, I spent the rest of that week on a high.

Three days later the fashion bomb went off in my wardrobe again as I tried on practically every single item of clothing I owned.

I called Juliet for a pep talk before I left.

'He likes you, Kate. What are you wearing?'

'Tight red trousers and a semi-sheer bodysuit with polka dots.'

'Gorgeous. How's your hair?'

I'd had Mikey cut it shorter and dye it a slightly lighter shade of brown just before the book signing.

'I've plaited it and tied it up a bit like Heidi.'

'I like it, demure but sexy.'

Feeling my plaits as I spoke, I shared my worries.

'Juliet, what if I make a fool of myself again?'

'You didn't make a fool of yourself, Kate. You just misjudged a situation and ended up kind of licking his face like a puppy.'

'God, Juliet, please don't say it out loud, I'm nervous enough as it is.'

I could hear her laughter at the other end of the line.

'I'm joking with you. Listen, Kate, you'll be fine and you'll have a great time. Remember James is one of the good guys. Your outfit sounds perfect, the venue is brilliant. Don't wind yourself up. You're just two young gorgeous people going out for some drinks and dinner. Relax and enjoy it.'

I set out towards Shoreditch and, arriving early, decided to wait for him inside the bar. Worried my nose had run in the cooling June evening, I made a beeline for the ladies, tidied myself up and popped in my eye drops. I knew we'd be eating later so I had brought a packet of crisps in my bag, which I ate to help open up the scar tissue in my throat. After the embarrassing finale of our first date, I didn't want this one to end with me choking at the table. Munching away, I wrestled in my bag until I found my sinus spray, which I use to help make it easier to breathe through my damaged nose – a must if we were going to kiss for real. I certainly wasn't going to be instigating it this time, but if he did, at least I'd be able to breathe.

I checked my teeth for remnants of crisps and made my way back into the bar. Surveying the room, I considered where to sit. I wanted a view of the door so I could see when he walked in, but I didn't want to be right in front of it in case other people recognised me and started asking me if I was that 'acid girl'. I picked a seat at the bar, making sure I wasn't directly underneath a light, and ordered a vodka and tonic. Two men next to me, about the same age as my dad, started chatting to me, I guess taking pity on the fact that I was there alone. Grateful for the distraction, I made polite small talk, before it suddenly occurred to me they probably thought I was a hooker.

'So what are you doing here all alone?' They asked.

'I'm waiting for someone . . . a friend.'

I couldn't say 'my boyfriend' – it was only our second date. What if he came in and they started talking to him and let slip that I'd said we were a couple?

'You're a pretty girl to be out at night on your own . . .'

'Ha . . . ahem . . . Oh thanks.'

I looked around nervously, willing James to walk in and rescue me. I checked my phone and saw a text from him.

'I'm so sorry, Kate, I'm running late, I'm getting there as fast as I can, am only a few minutes away.'

The men offered to buy me a drink.

'Oh thanks, but no I'm fine. I'm waiting for someone, honestly.'

'Go on, just one?'

They were harmless but I really didn't want them getting my drinks.

'I'll get my own but thank you very much for the offer.'

Ten minutes later I was still talking to them, unable to find a way to exit the conversation. I suppose I could have moved, but I didn't want to give up my perfect seat. My phone lit up with another text message.

'I'm here, where are you?'

I frantically texted back my location and craned my neck to see if he was coming through the door. A minute or two passed, so I texted again.

'I'm at the bar, by the right-hand wall as you look at it.'

His reply came back.

'What right-hand wall? You're in the Hoxton Hotel right?'

My stomach lurched. 'No, the Hoxton Grill,' I texted back.

I quickly scrolled back through our message history to see which one of us had got it wrong. I prayed it was him so I didn't have to walk out of here on my own. Another text.

'Oh God, Kate, I'm so sorry. My bad. I'll be there in a minute, am running . . . fast.'

I thought I'd be annoyed but I found it sweet and smiled at my phone. I was usually the one to mix things up, and besides, he'd admitted his error instantly rather than try to put the blame else-where, which I thought showed good character.

By the time James got to me, the guys I'd been chatting to had moved their attentions to a blonde further down the bar. James apologised profusely and we shared an awkward hug. I breathed in; he smelled fantastic.

We spent the entire night laughing, and ended up ordering shots. We only stopped when the bar started to close; we were both more than a bit tipsy. The nerves had gone and the awkwardness of the first date had been left far behind. The whole evening felt really relaxed and natural and as we got our coats to leave, James leaned in. This time I kept my head and waited until he'd definitely planted his lips on mine before I started kissing back. While I was completely captured by the moment, I couldn't help but breathe a mental sigh of relief. I hadn't messed it up, hadn't misread the signals, hadn't got it wrong. He liked me. James actually liked me enough to kiss me.

We went outside and he put me safely into a cab home. Waving goodbye, I watched his silhouette grow smaller and smaller through the back window of the taxi, hugging my bag tightly to my chest. By the time I got home to Chiswick, half an hour later, my cheeks were sore from smiling.

Chapter Sixteen

About a fortnight later, I was at the Foundation when I had a call from Josie, one of the PAs at Sony who I'd met through Simon Cowell.

'Hey, Katie, do you want some tickets for the Coldplay concert at the Emirates Stadium on Friday?'

'Wow, yes, that'd be fantastic! Are you sure?'

'Yes of course. Get there about 5pm, you've got my number, call me when you arrive and I'll tell you where to go for the tickets. Looking forward to seeing you.'

'Thanks, that's really, really generous.'

Things had been going brilliantly between James and me, so later that night I gave him a call. 'What are you up to this Friday?'

I held my breath, hoping he was free.

'Nothing really, what about you?'

Phew! We weren't quite at the stage yet where we presumed we'd get together on the weekends, so I was glad he was going to be around.

'Do you want to go to a concert? Do you like Coldplay?'

'Yeah, I really like them.'

'A friend has got some spare tickets. Want to come with me?'

'Yeah, that'd be great!'

This time it took me marginally less time to get ready, but only just. I settled on a pair of black leggings with black high heels and a loose, sleeveless, denim shirt that came to just above my knees. I'd cut the arms off it myself.

James met me off the train and we made our way to the stadium. I called Josie as we approached.

'Hi Katie, your tickets are waiting for you at the box office. Pick them up and then come up the stairs on the left-hand side and I'll meet you there.'

We collected the tickets and walked up the stairs to find nothing but a VIP door ahead of us. I looked around, presuming we'd gone the wrong way. I was about to turn back down the stairs when Josie opened the door.

'Katie, so good to see you! Come in, come in.'

She handed us both VIP passes. We looked at one another and shrugged, somewhat perplexed. I had no idea what to say and neither did James.

Josie excused herself for a minute, so James and I headed to the bar. We tried to pay for our drinks but someone explained that everything was free. As we stood there, making small talk, I really wanted to let him know I had no idea what was going on. I didn't want him to think I was showing off. But before I could open my mouth to explain, Josie reappeared.

'Katie, Chris wants to meet you. Follow me.'

My mind was racing as we followed her. Chris? Who was Chris? Not *Chris Martin*, surely? If it *was* him, what on earth would I say to him?

I could feel myself start to get hot and sweaty.

We entered a dressing room and, sure enough, there he was. Chris bloody Martin. *The* Chris Martin. He extended his hand to shake mine, like we did this every day. I was speechless, but thankfully he spoke first.

'Hi Katie, lovely to meet you. I saw your documentary. It really had an impact on me.'

I couldn't believe this was happening, that Chris Martin knew who I was. I looked to James to gauge his reaction: I could tell he was stunned but was styling it out with a bemused expression on his face.

'Thanks, Chris. That's really kind of you. Thank you.'

'A close member of my family was burned as a child, and I think the work you do at the Foundation is incredibly important. I know Simon Cowell is involved. How does he help you? How can I help you? What do you do at the charity?'

I explained that Simon came on board as patron of the Foundation when I set it up. He gave his support whenever and however I needed it; he was as active as his schedule allowed and was always there at key events to offer support and help raise the profile of the charity.

I told Chris about some of the things we work on at the Foundation, such as our workshops, scar management and camouflage make-up, and told him about the Scar Academy we were organising. We chatted for a while and I was struck not only by how funny and casual he was, but also by his openness and honesty. It felt genuine when he said he wanted to help. Then he switched his attention from me to James.

'So what is it you do with all your muscles?

James smiled and suddenly became really self-conscious of his tight T-shirt.

'Me? I'm . . . I'm Katie's friend.'

'Yes. Yep. He's my friend. This is James. My friend. *Friend.*'

I sounded like a complete idiot. But before the atmosphere could get any more awkward, the dressing room door opened and I did a double-take.

'Hi, I'm Gwyneth, it's a pleasure to meet you.'

I put my hand out. It was Gwyneth Paltrow. I tried not to stare but couldn't help it. She was beautiful.

'Hi, hello, pleased to meet you too.'

It was one of the most surreal moments of my life. We chatted for a while and then Chris introduced me to their children and we wished him luck before heading off to take our seats for the gig.

I still wanted to explain to James that I'd had no idea any of this was going to happen, but as we sat down he turned to me and spoke first.

'How unbelievable was that?'

'I know! Tell me about it.'

I breathed a sigh of relief. He took my hand and, as we watched the supporting act, I realised I didn't need to explain anything. James hadn't presumed I was out to impress.

It turned out to be one of the most amazing nights ever. At the end, fireworks lit up the sky, and that night Coldplay's 'Paradise' became 'our' song. Looking up at the stars as the music played it felt (in a North London football stadium kind of way!) that I was on my way to true happiness. After a few more dates, James and I had become exclusive.

Chapter Seventeen

I'd been trying to find the right time to introduce James to Mum and Dad. They knew about him and he knew I went over to theirs every Sunday for lunch. During the week we both worked really hard and rarely got the chance to see one another, which made our weekends together all the more important. So a week after the Coldplay gig I plucked up the courage to ask him to join me and my family for our Sunday lunch so we didn't have to spend the weekend apart. He said yes straight away. I texted Mum, asking her to set an extra place at the table.

It went off without a hitch. James was polite, gracious and appreciative. I felt far more relaxed than I'd thought I would and Dad warmed to him straight away. I called Mum as soon as I'd dropped James home and got back to my flat. I was dying to know what they thought.

'Well?'

'He seems nice. Dad likes him.'

'I knew they'd get on. James reminds me a bit of him. He's a really nice guy, don't you think?'

I wanted their blessing so much. Things felt just right with James and I hoped they would see he was good for me.

'Yes, he's very well mannered and seems lovely.'

'I know it's early days, Mum, but I think he's perfect.'

'Just don't get hurt Kate, okay?'

'I promise, Mum.'

Then she said the magic words. 'Feel free to bring him with you again next Sunday.'

It was the approval I needed.

After our Coldplay experience, I started opening up more about my work life. I told James about my new book, the TV stuff and the awards ceremonies I went to. So when I was contacted by The London Organising Committee of the Olympic and Paralympic Games and asked to help light the Paralympic flame, James was one of the first people I called. It was one of the biggest honours of my life and I wanted him to share it with me.

'Can you come? Mum and Dad and Suze will definitely be there so I won't be alone, and I know you're manic at work so I completely understand if you can't make it.'

What he said next made my heart soar.

'Kate, I wouldn't miss it for the world. I'll be there.'

The organisers told me that I would carry the English torch into the lighting ceremony at Stoke Mandeville Hospital, together with Paralympian and thirty-eight-time medal winner Tony Griffin, and alongside other runners carrying the Welsh, Scottish and Northern Irish torches. Our combined torches would then light the Paralympic flame, which would go on a twenty-four-hour relay from Buckinghamshire to London, and ultimately to open the Paralympic Games.

There was just one little thing . . . While I wouldn't have missed this opportunity for the world, since the attack I've been completely petrified of fire, and of anything with the potential to burn me. I dug deep and told myself that it would all be okay. We did a practice run on the day and I was fine with the unlit torch, but the minute the burning flame was handed to me I froze. It didn't help that I had to run with the torch right by my head on a windy day. Inside I was freaking out a little.

But the strength of human spirit that was around me was amazing and gave me the confidence I needed. There were so many inspirational people there that day, people who'd overcome such challenges. The Scottish flame was carried by Noel McShane, who'd set up the National Wheelchair Tennis Association of Great Britain, and by Jon Jo Look, a boxer who'd lost his leg in an accident and broken his hand in fourteen places, but was boxing again and coaching young athletes. The Northern Irish flame was carried by Darren Ferguson, a Special Police Constable who, despite being a volunteer, had won special recognition for talking down a suicidal man from a bridge, and by Joseph Morris, who had saved a girl from drowning in a river. Marsha Wiseman and Julie Gilbert carried the Welsh torch; they were part of a team of champion disabled athletes who all work for BT.

And, of course, Mum, Dad, Suzy and James were all there to watch, too, as promised. Dad was armed with his camera and couldn't have been prouder as he hugged me.

'How you feeling, Kate? Nervous?'

'Just a bit, Dad.'

Suzy could see I needed a confidence boost.

'You'll be fine and you will do a great job. Hey, it's not like the world is watching or anything.'

'Ha, ha. Thanks very much. What if the torch sets my hair on fire? I've got loads of hairspray in it.'

'It won't, sis, you'll be fine. You look fantastic so just concentrate on what this means and how important a day it is. Just think: if you have kids one day you'll be able to tell them you were part of London 2012 and that you helped to light the Paralympic flame! You're part of history, Kate. Not everyone gets to say that.'

'Oh my God, as if I wasn't nervous enough.'

I knew she was right, and that I had to do this. With a big smile, I ran as fast as I could without it looking odd.

My part of the relay was over in just a few short minutes. I came out unscathed and as the torch was carried further away into the distance, I felt flushed with relief and pride.

I loved being part of something that was so diverse and that celebrated triumph over adversity on an international stage. James gave me a huge hug as Mum, Dad and Suzy crowded round. I hugged him back as Suzy piped up,

'See? Your hair wasn't in any danger of being set alight at any time.'

We all laughed. Dad took out his camera and snapped a picture of us all together.

I spent the next week watching the games, which was hugely inspiring. And I even managed to get James and me tickets for the closing ceremony. As we watched a million lights moving along to Coldplay playing our song, 'Paradise', I felt tingly with goosebumps at just how perfectly things were starting to fall into place.

Chapter Eighteen

After the excitement of the Paralympics, I threw myself into work at the Foundation and for Channel 4 – I had been asked to take part in a new five-part series, *Secret Millions*. The channel was working with The Big Lottery Fund to make £10 million available for radical social schemes, and each week a celebrity and a charity were paired up to test out progressive new ideas for positive change and to try to win funding. Gok Wan, Jimmy Doherty, Dave Fishwick and George Clarke were also taking part.

For my episode, I would work with the Acumen Trust, who find paid work for ex-convicts once they have been released to reduce the temptation and need to reoffend. Together we would help start a back-to-work scheme which would teach former offenders how to make and sell high-end furniture. The show would document how important rehabilitation is for inmates, both during and after their sentences.

Because I was such a high-profile crime victim, the channel felt I could bring a unique perspective to the programme. Though I was terrified at the thought of meeting convicted criminals who might be like the men who attacked me, I'd already spent recent months pushing myself outside of my comfort zone, so I focused on this as an opportunity to learn and challenge myself further. I also knew the channel was sensitive to my fears and wouldn't let me come to any harm. Still, I had some time before the filming started to get myself mentally prepared. It was a big thing to consider.

At the Foundation I was working on our second celebrity fundraising ball, in addition to Scar Academy, which would take place in a few months' time. It was already getting great support and our patron Simon Cowell had promised to attend. He had bought a bunch of tickets for his friends and was doing everything he could to help.

I was also scheduled to give a talk at the Brit Mums conference, which is held every year in London for mums who blog. My mum means the world to me, so giving a bit back by speaking to a room full of mums felt special and poignant.

Even though I often found it hard to talk to individual strangers or journalists in detail about what happened to me, I have always felt much more comfortable being open about the attack when I give talks to larger groups, and I rarely get nervous. Standing behind a podium I always feel in charge of what I have to say.

I asked James and Mum to come with me. James hadn't heard me speak in public yet, but I wanted him to know what all aspects of my life were like. As I shuffled my bits of paper and began the familiar opening to my speech, I suddenly felt on the verge of tears. Knowing James was there made me feel more nervous than I expected. Seeing him sat there beside my mum, I felt overwhelmed with emotions towards both of them. I hoped nobody would notice, and pushed on.

'Good afternoon everyone and thank you for coming today.'

I opened by telling them about what happened to me four years before.

'Standing here in this room this afternoon and saying these words out loud to you, I still can't believe this actually happened. But this isn't a story of misery. This is a story of how strong the mind really can be when using the power of positive thinking. You can survive without food for three weeks, without water for three days and you can survive without air for three minutes. But you cannot survive without hope, and this is the story of how I held on to hope . . .'

As I spoke about my darkest hours to this room full of mothers, I couldn't take my eyes off my own. Clicking through pictures taken during my recovery, I thought about how everything I'd achieved so far was thanks to her patience, diligence, love and unflinching support and belief in me. With my voice breaking and a tear falling down my cheek, I felt overwhelmed with gratitude towards her for helping me get this far. Everyone around me knows how much my mum means to me, and so many people who have watched my documentary say how remarkable they found her. And that's exactly what she is, my remarkable mum.

I got a standing ovation when I finished. Afterwards, Mum, James and I went for lunch and talked about the event. It made me so happy to have them with me and while I'd have loved to have spent the rest of the afternoon with them both, it was one of those crazy days and I had to rush off to a TV production meeting, so I kissed them both and jumped in a cab as soon as we'd finished dessert.

I emerged three hours later to one of the most ill-timed phone calls I've ever received. It was from my doctor's PA, telling me that a date had been scheduled for my next operation, which was to try to reduce some contracted scar issue. This time it was for my nose, which had been sore for weeks. The grafted tissue on it, which originally came from my back, had started to shrink. Ear cartilage had been used in an attempt to widen my nostrils, but it was weaker than the retracting skin, which was starting to pull my top lip up and my nose back into my face. Unless treated, my lip would slowly continue to move up and my nose would become flat and virtually non-existent. I'd had a consultation at the hospital a few days previously and was waiting to hear what the plan was.

My doctor, Mr Dunaway, confirmed I'd need another graft.

'Katie, in due course we'll need to take stronger cartilage from your ribs to reconstruct your nose, but before we do that we need to see if we can stretch some of your grafted skin to cover what we're planning to do.'

He explained I'd have to use what's called an osmosis expander. It's the size of a grain of rice and made of self-inflating gel tissue. It would be implanted under the grafted skin on my nose and would grow to about five times its original size in four days, thereby helping the skin to stretch. Under normal circumstances, it expands and stretches the skin like pregnancy does to the tummy, and makes it possible for your own skin to cover the graft or reconstruction by the time you go into theatre . . . *Under normal circumstances.*

My doctor made it abundantly clear as he inserted the expander a few days later that it was hard to tell how my scarred tissue would react. My nose started aching the second he'd finished but he reminded me to keep a close eye on how my skin grew over the next few days since they didn't know what the expansion rate on grafted skin would be and it might actually split.

Two days later I woke up with a throbbing nose. Clambering out of bed and into the bathroom I turned on the shower before seeing my reflection and letting out a yelp.

There was a hole about the size of a pea near the tip of my nose, where the tissue expander had torn through the grafted skin. What remained was purple and swollen.

It looked awful. I immediately panicked – James was supposed to be coming over that night to watch a movie and get a take-away.

I called Suzy, who is always good in a crisis. She'd know what to do.

'You've got to help me think of an excuse so I don't have to see James tonight. He knows about the operations and knows I've got the expander in but I don't want him to see this side of my life this early, the complications bit where things go wrong. I don't want to take the risk and scare him off.'

'Why not? Maybe now's the time to show him things aren't always plain sailing and let him make up his own mind?'

I knew she had a point but I wasn't sure either of us was ready for that.

'Seriously? What am I supposed to say? "Just ignore the huge hole in my nose and give us a kiss?" '

'Well you don't have to put it quite . . .'

I interrupted her before she'd finished.

'Suze, there's snot coming from the hole, this is a nightmare! I can't ask him to deal with all of this, it's too soon . . .'

Cancelling or changing the procedure wasn't an option. After all, this was my reality, a reality anyone who wanted to be with me was going to have to accept. But I was still wearing matching underwear for him, for goodness sake, and here I was, eight hours away from seeing him, with what felt like a gigantic crater in my nose.

One trip to the hospital later and I was loaded up with antibiotics to make sure it didn't get infected. I called James to cancel our night in, telling him what had happened.

'I'm a bit tired, I don't think I'm up for tonight.'

'I'll just come over for as long as you want me, then I'll head off. I want to make sure you're okay.'

'I'm fine, honest.'

'Kate, I'm coming. I have a DVD and will see you at 8pm.'

I was desperate to keep him away but he seemed determined to come.

By the time he knocked on the door, I could feel my nose swelling even more. He knew what had happened but I wasn't sure he properly understood just how bad it was, so I'd turned down the lights to make it as subtle as possible.

'Hey, how was your day?'

'Great, busy but good, how was yours? How's your nose?'

He gave me a kiss on the cheek, kicked off his shoes and hung up his jacket.

'Yeah, you know . . . not bad.'

He gathered me up in a hug and rested his chin on the top of my head.

'Right, I have three movies to choose from, so I say we stretch our legs a little, pop out and get some ice cream from the shop and then come back and chill.'

His suggestion filled me with dread.

I know what it's like having people whisper and point and laugh. He didn't. There was no way I was exposing him to that this early on.

'I don't really fancy ice cream.'

He looked at me.

'Has someone snatched the real Kate? You always fancy ice cream.'

'No, not tonight. You can get some if you like but I'm alright.'

'Come too so I don't get the wrong flavour.'

I knew he was pushing for me to go with him for all the right reasons, but I could feel myself starting to get hot and sweaty at the prospect.

'James, maybe I don't want to go out?'

'Why? It's only a quick trip to the shop, we'll be back watching a movie within fifteen minutes.'

'I'll stay here and get the movie set up, you go.'

I was running out of excuses but desperate not to step outside.

'Come on, I'll even throw in a chocolate bar.'

'I don't think you want you to be seen out with me like this, James.'

This made him pause.

'What? Why?'

'I don't want you to be embarrassed.'

'Why would I be embarrassed, Kate?'

I gestured at the huge hole in my nose.

'Look at me. I look a total state. Everyone will stare at me, then they'll stare at you and wonder what you're doing with the freak. They'll try to figure out whether you're my brother or carer or boyfriend, then they'll start talking behind their hands and staring at you and pointing. I'm used to it. You're not. It's not a nice feeling. And I don't want you to be bothered by it.'

I looked down at the floor. James came close and gently lifted my chin so I'd look at him. He gave me a reassuring smile.

'I don't care, let them stare, we're getting ice cream. They're free to stare and we're free to ignore them. It's a free country and that's that, okay?'

He grabbed his coat and threw me mine. I turned my back to him while I put it on, wiping the tears that were forming in the corners of my eyes. It was what I'd longed to hear for years. The moment I never thought would come. Finally, someone who was proud to be with me and didn't care what other people thought when they looked at me. Someone who wanted to walk with me to the supermarket to get ice cream despite the fact my nose looked like I'd slammed it in a door. Several doors, in fact.

In that second, I realised James was doing what I'd always worried was impossible: looking beyond the surface to what was inside me. He'd done it naturally, with no effort, no sob story, no back story on my part. He liked me just how he met me. Not perfect, just Kate.

Chapter Nineteen

By the time Paul's wedding rolled around a month later at the start of September, my nose had healed and I looked a lot less bruised and battered. I'd never been a bridesmaid before, but, as Paul reminded me, I loved dressing up so what better excuse was there than his wedding? Leah's sisters were bridesmaids too, so there'd be four of us altogether including Suzy.

So much had changed since I went out to visit Paul and Leah in 2011. I'd thought about asking James to come with us but it wasn't like it was a short drive along the M4 to a small family wedding in Hampshire. Paul was getting married in Colorado, nearly five thousand miles away, so it would cost a lot for James to find a flight at such short notice and would have meant him taking time off work when he was really busy, not to mention we'd have to reconfigure the hotel rooms we'd booked for Suzy and me to share. I said goodbye to him the night before we left and promised I'd text him.

Paul and Leah were waiting for us in the arrivals hall. I rushed over, dropped my bags on the floor and gave them both a huge hug. I couldn't resist quizzing Paul about his impending nuptials.

'Feeling nervous yet?'

'Nope, not a bit. How's things with you?'

Suzy broke us apart, giving him a squeeze herself. 'She's great, she's got a boyfriend . . .'

'Suze . . .!' I protested.

'Mum told me – James, right?' It was clear there were no secrets in our family.

'Yep.'

Paul winked at me and smiled.

'Told you things would work out, didn't I? Maybe you'll be next down the aisle.'

The following few days passed in a blur of happy excitement. As we ran around getting a few last-minute things for the big day, as well as decorating the venue, we spent quality time together as a family. It was great not having all the attention on me for a change; we weren't preparing for an operation or attending a work event, we were there to celebrate Paul and Leah. The wedding was all about them and I loved every single second of it.

We'd all booked to stay in the hotel where the wedding was taking place and spent hours getting ready together when the big day arrived. I helped Leah with her hair and then joined Mum and Suzy to get ready. Leah and the other bridesmaids had monopolised their room so Paul was with us. He and Dad barely got a look in in the bathroom with three women hogging it. We also got a sneak preview of Paul's speech for the reception as he gave it one last practice run. We all wished him luck in his last few hours as a bachelor before making our way to the ceremony as a family. As bridesmaids, we'd be walking up the aisle first followed by Leah.

As I took some last-minute deep breaths before the ceremony was due to start, Leah's aunt and uncle tapped my arm.

'We just wanted to say we've been praying for you ever since we heard your story from Paul and it's an honour to finally meet you.'

I'd been feeling emotional all morning anyway and their lovely words, on this, the biggest day of their niece's life, instantly made my eyes brim with tears. The kindness of strangers has always overwhelmed me and, thankfully, always gives me strength. Taking a deep breath and pulling myself together, I cleared my throat, thanked them and waited for the music to begin.

The ceremony was incredibly emotional. Suzy and I walked up the aisle beaming at Paul, who looked fantastic and so happy. Suzy and I then stood to the side holding our flowers and faced the congregation. Watching Leah walk towards her future husband, my brother, I felt a lump form in my throat.

During the ceremony I couldn't take my eyes off Mum and Dad in the front row. I watched them wipe their eyes as their eldest child said his vows. I knew their tears weren't just those of happiness for Paul; they were for all of us: for them, for Suzy, me, Paul and Leah. For the happy, contented life we all shared now, which just a few years before, when I was in intensive care, we weren't always sure we'd reach.

We all shed more tears at the reception. Paul's speech was funny and heart-warming; he talked about how Leah had given him confidence and made him believe in himself. He talked about their future and what love meant to them both, adding, 'Leah is the partner I thought I would never find and when I did find her, I knew my search was over.' Then Leah sang Etta James's 'At Last', and there wasn't a dry eye in the house.

But they had one more surprise up their sleeves. Their first dance was a slow one but just after it started, the CD scratched and they lost the sound. We all looked at one another, gutted for them that the first dance of their married lives had been ruined. Then, 'Gangnam Style' came on. Without missing a beat, Paul pulled two pairs of luminous sunglasses from his pocket, handed one pair to Leah, and they executed a hilarious and fantastically choreographed dance. They had everyone up on their feet by the end, and when we all rushed up to hug them after the song finished, Paul sheepishly admitted they'd been having dance lessons. Suzy was the most gobsmacked of us all.

'Leah, what have you done with our brother?'

Leah let out a huge laugh, 'Bet you didn't know he had the moves, eh?'

Suzy turned to Paul.

'Seriously, you spent thirty-six years trying to go unnoticed, and here you are busting moves on your wedding day!'

It was an amazing night, and the whole time I was there I couldn't stop thinking about James. Seeing love first-hand between Paul and Leah, and knowing they'd be together forever, made me think about my own relationship. I knew it was early days but it felt secure. Felt right. Felt normal. I prayed it would stay that way. Prayed that I wouldn't mess it up or ruin it.

When I got back to my room, I hung up my dress and crawled into bed after entirely too many hours in high heels. I texted James, telling him all about the day and that I wished he was with me. Despite the time difference, he texted straight back.

'Me too, night gorgeous xxx'

As I fell asleep, that line from Paul's speech replayed over and over in my head, about Leah being the partner he thought he'd never find and his search being over. I felt elated that with James I might also have finally found the happiness I'd been longing for. But I was scared of the nagging vulnerability I was starting to feel, which came with the possibility of opening my heart to love.

Chapter Twenty

When I got home from Colorado, I decided to surprise James with a weekend away in Liverpool to make up for our time apart. We caught the train up after work on the Friday, and spent the night bar-hopping and drinking cocktails. After dinner and shots, we got back to our hotel around 2am, but I wasn't ready for bed.

'Shall I order a bottle of champagne from room service?'

He looked at me quizzically. 'Seriously? Let's just go to bed.'

'Oh come on, James, it's still early. It'll be fun. Let's get some fizz.'

'Nah, Kate, we've got an early train tomorrow, we should get some sleep.'

I was having a good time and didn't want our night to end. I have no idea why, but in that split second something in my mind turned and I completely overreacted. Instead of seeing him as the guy I fancied, the nice guy that he was, I suddenly saw him – unfairly – as the guy who was trying to put an end to my fun. The vulnerability I'd been feeling charged straight to the surface like a torpedo and my thinking changed in a heartbeat.

I shot back at him.

'You please yourself, I'm going to order some champagne anyway.'

'Really? Come on, we've both had enough. Bedtime, Kate? Please? It'll be a waste of money to get more.'

To this day I still don't know exactly what happened in my head. It was probably a fatal combination of putting myself under undue pressure to have the 'perfect' relationship after witnessing Paul's wedding, and having too much to drink that night. I had suddenly become wracked with insecurity that I wasn't good enough for James, and that it was only a matter of time before he decided he didn't want to be with me and broke my heart.

In reality, none of that was true. In fact what we had was the total opposite; we'd grown so close, he deserved my trust, and I was giving him more and more of my vulnerable heart. But there in the hotel room something snapped back, and my self-preservation kicked in big time. I felt I'd be better off pushing him away before he had the chance to do the same to me. My paranoid anger, which had been buried somewhere deep down, had come flowing to the top. Hurtful words started tumbling out of my mouth like water from a burst pipe.

'Get off my back, okay? You don't own me, you're not my boss. I can do whatever the hell I want.'

He looked at me like I'd just slapped him in the face.

'Hey, calm down. I'm not trying to be anything. I just think we've both had enough to drink and it's 2am. Come to bed, Kate. Please. Don't turn what's been a lovely night into something else.'

I barely let him finish before I said the coldest words that I still can't believe came out of my mouth.

'Don't tell me what to do, James. I don't need you, I don't need anyone. Just leave me alone. I don't want you.'

I don't remember what happened next but I woke up the following morning with a blinding hangover, still fully dressed and him wide awake beside me with a worried look on his face.

'So, Kate . . . What are we going to do?'

'Hmmm? What?'

'Last night. Did you mean what you said about me? About us? About our future?'

I tried to remember what I had said but my head was still fuzzy. 'Huh? I was drunk, let's go get something to eat, I'm starving.'

I started to sit up in bed and he gently touched my arm.

'Kate, hang on. You said you wanted to be alone, that you didn't want anything to do with me.'

My head was pounding, and the fear and worry written all over his face nearly brought me to tears. I sat staring at him as my eyes adjusted to daylight, thinking a million things and not being able to say any of them. I wanted to tell him he was amazing, the best thing that had happened to me since the attack. I wanted to tell him he was perfect and that I'd been an idiot. I wanted to tell him I was scared and hadn't trusted anyone with my heart since before the attack and had forgotten how to. But all I got out was, 'I need a shower.'

I stood under the warm water, wondering what the hell I had done. Why had I tried to push away the first person I'd actually cared for in ages, and who clearly cared for me? Why had I been so vicious to him?

I was so ashamed. We breakfasted in near-silence and made small talk most of the journey home, but I finally worked up the nerve to apologise. He accepted it instantly and because he didn't ask for an explanation, I didn't offer one. The truth was I had no idea why it had happened, it had just come out and I could barely control it. I think now that maybe I manufactured an argument just to see how much he *really* cared. To test how far I could push him away and still have him come back to me. It was a dangerous game, and it wasn't fair to either of us.

He was his remarkable, forgiving self. 'Don't worry about it, Kate.'

'Yeah, I am sorry though, James. Really I am. I don't know . . .'

'Forget about it; it's fine, honestly.'

He held my hand and I knew I was lucky to be forgiven.

But rather than learn from my mistake, it marked the start of a very negative pattern in our fledgling relationship. A few weeks later, after what was supposed to be a quiet night in, I found myself sobbing uncontrollably after having again drunk too much, telling him we couldn't be together, that I was never going to get over what had happened to me. I was a mess, make-up running down my face as I cried that I was better off alone. He gathered me up in a hug. I was so worked up I could barely take in what he was saying.

'You will get over it because I'm here and I'll help you. I promise you I'll stick by you and we'll move forward together. I'll be here to help you.'

'No you won't. I know you won't be because I can't be with you, I'm not supposed to have a boyfriend. It's too difficult. Look at me. No one was ever supposed to love me. You shouldn't stay with me. I'm not the girl you should be with.'

I dug out some pictures of me from before the attack: pretty, blonde and carefree, and pushed them into his hand.

'That's the girl you should have been with, not this one.'

He kept his eyes fixed on me, and didn't even glance at them.

'Why? I don't know that person, Kate. I know you.' He dropped the photos onto the table.

'What's the point of looking at these pictures of a stranger when it's you I want to be with?'

He was saying all the right things but I was wound up so tight. With a hanging head, he walked slowly to the bedroom, leaving me filled with fear and anger and no one to direct it at.

Waking up the next morning with another hangover, I rolled over, expecting James to be there beside me, but instead I found a note with my name on the front of it. I stared at it with dread, praying it didn't say what I thought it might – that he'd had enough, that I needed more help than he could provide, that he wanted to stay friends. I leaned over and picked it up, certain my world was about to turn on its head.

Hey, just popped back home to get some stuff sorted for work tomorrow, I'll be back tonight and we can go for dinner. J xx

I was shaking with relief.

I couldn't remember much of what had happened the night before, but seeing my old pictures lying on the table I knew I must have shown them to him. As I showered, pieces of the evening started coming back to me. With a crushing sense of embarrassment and humiliation, I dried off and got dressed. I started to clean up the flat, giving myself a talking to as I put on a wash.

'What the hell are you doing? You wanted a boyfriend. You wanted someone who could love you unconditionally and see what's on the inside. Well, now you've found him and you're pushing him away. You've got the chance of real happiness with James and you're messing it up. What's the matter with you, Kate?'

I stared at myself in the mirror, taking in my reflection for what felt like hours, psyching myself up to be completely open and honest with James when he got back that night. I'd tell him the truth about how scared I was to let him into my heart and mind. I would be honest about how I had probably been hiding behind alcohol in recent weeks so I didn't have to face up to the fact I was falling for him and was utterly terrified he'd break my heart and set back my still-ongoing recovery.

Six hours later, he knocked on the door. I tried to sound light and breezy.

'Hi, how was your day?'

'Yeah, fine thanks. How was yours?'

'Good. Fine. Great. Yeah. I'm sorry about last night but, sit down with me, I've got something to tell you . . .'

We moved to the sofa. I explained that I was scared, that I found it unfathomable that an amazing guy like him could want someone like me. I told him I hadn't been serious about anyone since the attack and that the growing feelings I had were new and terrifying. I told him the fear made me feel he'd be better off without me, and that maybe I really was meant to be alone as long as I had all these emotional issues to deal with from the attack.

We sat there looking at one another.

'But you're not alone, Kate, not anymore.'

He pulled me towards him.

'Don't worry, Kate, I'm here and I'm not going anywhere.'

'Really?'

'Really.'

Holding on to one another felt like a lifeline in the dark. Breathing in the smell of his shirt, I felt so lucky to have found someone who had let me make such huge mistakes so early on, and who still saw a glint of something despite my mistakes and still believed in me. Someone who knew I wasn't perfect, and who never demanded perfection.

His patience had shown me an alternative. How life can be when someone refuses to give up on you. How love can make you feel that anything is possible. I knew I had unconditional love from my family, but I needed this too in order to help get my life back to 'normal' and put the past behind me. James represented a big part of my fresh start in the world: he didn't have to be with me but he'd stuck around because he wanted to, because he thought I was worth it.

In the weeks that followed, I let him in more. And as my heart started to fill with happiness and trust, it overshadowed the fear that had taken a hold in there. I didn't want to fight or push him away anymore, I didn't need to test him to see if he'd keep coming back. It was much nicer to watch a movie together, go to bed and hold one another while we fell asleep.

I stopped drinking for a while too. It was no good as an emotional crutch and all it had done was exacerbate my emotions until they came tumbling out in a drunken, ranting, one-sided argument that I could never win.

The good feelings started to carry over into other areas of my life, and I was doing more healthy, productive things for myself. I'd wanted to hire a personal trainer for months so, turning over a new leaf, I not only booked a block of twenty sessions, I entered a half-marathon to give myself a goal. Every Saturday morning I'd leave James in bed to enjoy a lie-in as I pulled on my trainers and headed out to run. On my return, we'd go for breakfast before spending the day together. With our real foundations now bedding in, I started to realise I was falling in love with him. I'd asked friends what love felt like and the answer I'd always had was 'you just know'. I've doubted my judgement about many things in my life, but that 'knowing' feeling about James was undeniable.

Chapter Twenty-One

By the time the Royal Parks Half-Marathon came around at the end of October 2012, I was finally on the even keel I'd longed for when I moved to London three years previously. The Katie Piper Foundation was also moving forward, growing and adapting. Workshops, talks and mentoring schemes had spread all over the country, and we now had four hard-working, dedicated staff and a growth plan in place.

I'd been training hard for my run and as I compiled my Ministry of Sound playlist on the morning of the race, I was feeling excited to get out there and try my best. James, Mum and Suzy all came to the starting line to watch me set off.

As I pounded the pavement, people recognised me and cheered for me and I smiled and waved back. It was such an energy boost! James found me halfway along and shouted the encouraging words I needed to keep going and push myself over the line. Two hours and three minutes after I started, I crossed the finish line, having run through Hyde Park, Kensington Park, St James's Palace Gardens and Green Park. James, Mum and Suzy all gathered me in a group hug and I fell into their arms, exhausted but exhilarated.

James rushed off to get me something to eat but before he came back I was ushered onto the press table for interviews. While I was desperate to disappear and be with James and my family, it was the first time ever that I was being interviewed about something totally unrelated to the attack.

'Who's your running idol?'

'How did it feel crossing the line?'

'What's the atmosphere like out there today?'

'Will you try and do it faster next year?'

I loved it.

Resting my aching legs the next day, James and I lay on his bed watching TV. I was feeling warm, fulfilled and contented, and a lot of those feelings were down to James. We had been together over four months by that point and while I hadn't yet said the 'L' word out loud, I knew I felt it and I desperately hoped he felt the same. As I lay there mulling things over in my mind, he looked at me and started to speak, as if he knew what I was thinking.

'I'm really happy, Kate. The happiest I've been ever. I think we get on brilliantly. You're smart, funny, beautiful. And I want you to know I've fallen for you completely.'

My heart started pounding. I knew how *I* felt about *him* but after our first fateful half-kiss, I'd promised myself I wouldn't be the one to say 'I love you' first. I tried to phrase my next sentence as carefully as I could, letting him know how I felt without leaving myself open to embarrassment. I took a deep breath.

'I think I might be, maybe, falling in love with you, James . . .'

It said enough but didn't go full throttle just in case he didn't feel the same.

'I love you too . . .'

We both burst out laughing and I playfully whacked him, adding:

'Hey, you made me say it first, that's cheating.'

He wrapped me up in a hug.

'Yeah, you said it first but I probably meant it first.'

I felt an overwhelming sense of peace. Nestling into his shoulder, in my head I chalked up another victory over my attackers. I was loved! It seemed as good a time as any to bring up something that had been playing on my mind for the last month.

'James?'

'Yeah.'

'I've been thinking about house hunting for a bigger place . . .'

'I thought you loved West London?'

He was right, and I was also a little attached to the first home I'd lived in on my own, but I was ready for something more.

'I do but my flat is pretty poky. And you know how I feel about security; I don't even have off-street parking where I am now. I'm working long hours at the charity and I know it's good being so close to the offices but I've been thinking about formalising my hours there, not running there at 10pm on a Thursday night to put in a few hours just because it's down the road and I can. Moving further away will probably help me get some structure.'

'So where would you move?'

'I don't know, I've been having a bit of a look at Surrey and Kent but they're both too expensive.'

I was still resting on his shoulder and he shifted round so he could look me in the eyes.

'You could have a look round here in East London? I mean "we" could have a look round here. Just if you wanted to?'

I could have sworn he just asked me to move in with him.

'I'd like to. Would you like to?'

'Yeah. Yes. Living together would make more sense, I've been thinking we're too far away from one another. We could start looking this weekend.'

I still couldn't believe what I was hearing.

'I'll need to put my flat on the market, but it'd be good to start looking at places together wouldn't it?'

'Yes, Kate, especially now we're in love.'

I giggled and whacked him again and resumed my place on his shoulder. It was all so easy, so simple and pure. We spent the rest of the night scouring the internet for properties and over the next few weeks emailed each other constantly with places we wanted to look at. We were in love and we wanted to live together. It had all happened so fast, and I knew the next step wouldn't happen overnight, but just knowing we were moving in the same direction and wanted the same things was all I needed.

I was still deliriously happy when Kay got in touch a few days later. I'd been in meetings and had a few missed calls from her. I hoped it wasn't anything worrying and I dialled her number.

'Hey, Tiny. I wanted you to be the first to know.'

'Know what?'

My mind went into overdrive. She was already engaged so it wasn't that. I knew they were still planning the wedding and hadn't set a date. I started panicking something bad had happened to her but then remembered. Of course, she'd been trying for a baby.

'I'm pregnant . . .'

'You're what?!'

She started laughing and I did too.

'I'm having a baby, Kate! Don't tell anyone else, I'm not three months yet. I just couldn't wait to tell you.'

'Oh. My. God. Kay. I'm so happy for you. SO happy. What, when, I mean . . . How far along are you?'

'Seven weeks.'

'You're going to be a mum, Kay! I'm so happy for you. You're going to be a mum, with a real baby!'

'I know . . .'

I was filled with joy for her. Genuine, pure joy. She had shared such special news with me so I shared mine with her too. Kay was delighted, as I knew she would be. While we didn't say it out loud, I knew we both felt we'd reached huge milestones in our lives. Kay had been with me through so much, helped and nurtured me more than she could ever know and now we were each moving towards new chapters in our lives. New beginnings. We spent ages on the phone, celebrating one another's happiness.

I had another big missed call that month. I was in a production meeting with Channel 4 a few weeks later when my phone flashed a call from Mags, the lady who has handled my publicity ever since we met while filming my first documentary. I made a mental note to call her back from the cafe across the street.

'Hi Mags, sorry I missed you. Is everything okay?'

'Katie, are you sitting down?'

My breath caught in my throat and my hands started to feel clammy. I instantly began to look around me, petrified she was going to tell me Danny and Stefan had escaped from prison and were on their way to get me.

'Mags, what is it . . .? What? Tell me now.'

'Are you ready for this? You've won a Pride of Britain Award.'

'What? Who has?'

I couldn't have heard her correctly.

'You, Katie.'

'I don't understand, what do you mean?'

I could still hear my heart pumping in my ears but the gut-wrenching fear in my stomach had given way to butterflies. I finally did as Mags asked and sat down.

'It's a special recognition award for all the work you've done through the Foundation, for setting it up and making such a difference to so many people. You won. You won you won you won!'

Mags was squealing and could barely contain her excitement but for me it all seemed so unreal.

'I don't get it. Do I have to talk about the attack?'

'No, no. Katie this is about here and now and the future, not the past. It's just for your work in the charity world. Nothing to do with the past.'

'Oh my God. I've never been given an award for anything other than being burned and, you know, being attacked and not dying. Isn't it for everyone at the charity?'

'It's just for you but they've filmed everyone at the charity and now they want to film you for a clip to be shown on the awards night.'

Now it was my turn to let out a squeal.

'What? They filmed with everyone at the charity and they all kept it secret?'

It was completely overwhelming.

I took Suzy on a mammoth shopping trip to find something special to wear to the ceremony and spent hours trying on a million different dresses. It was still a couple of months away but I wanted to get a head start. I knew I wanted to wear something long but wasn't sure about colour. I finally settled on a black, one-shoul-dered dress with ruching and a jewelled brooch on the waist. After examining myself from every angle I whipped open the dressing-room curtain to find Suzy sitting on the floor checking her phone.

'This says classy, successful, charitable, demure and happy, right?'

'Yes, Kate, it does. However, so did the previous five.'

'Shall I try them again? I like this one best but if you're not sure . . .?'

She looked up at me in exasperation.

'Kate, you look fantastic. But seriously, as much as I love shop-ping, if you want to try any more dresses on, I'm going to have to get a sleeping bag and have a nap.'

'I just want to look perfect . . . If you know what I mean.'

She took a deep breath, put her phone in her pocket and stood up.

'The one-shoulder looks sexy but not too sexy, the length says "demure", the colour says "professional" and the detail says "young and fashionable". I really think you might have "the dress".'

'And you're not just saying that because you want to go home?'

'While you're right on one count – I do desperately want to go home – I honestly, hand-on-heart swear to God that I think that dress is perfect. Why don't we go home and decide what to do with your hair . . .'

'Oh my God, my hair! I hadn't even thought about that.'

As I rushed to pay, I saw Suzy smiling. She swung her bag over her shoulder and followed me out.

I usually love doing my own hair and make-up but I knew on the night of the awards I'd be all thumbs, so I made sure that I booked a hair and make-up artist well in advance who would pamper me and get me ready on the day so that I could just try to relax.

I had also been told that I could bring a few guests with me to the ceremony at the Grosvenor Hotel, so I invited Mum, Dad, Suzy, James and Mr Jawad. James and I had been together nearly six months by the time the awards came around but I still wanted to keep him secret from the press. I didn't want him to see head-lines like 'Acid Girl Finds Love', and he was happy staying out of the limelight. While there's a lot of my life I'm willing to make public, there are some things that are nice to keep private for as long as possible, so he and Suzy were on strict orders to pretend they were a couple.

They all came up the red carpet with me and while I was pulled aside for pictures I couldn't keep from glancing back and smiling that my family, my doctor and saviour, and my true love were all there with me on such a big night. The only person missing was Paul, but Suzy made sure she texted him lots of pictures of the event.

I was feeling the nerves as we were shown to our table. Mum and Dad sat next to one another, Mr Jawad sat next to Dad, then there was me, then Amanda Holden and her friend, then Gok Wan, Gok's friend, and 'lovebirds' Suzy and James.

I was on edge all evening. I could barely concentrate and kept going to the toilet to check my hair and make-up. When the room fell dark to watch my tape, I could feel a lump start in my throat.

They'd interviewed burns survivors I'd worked with. People I'd met in the early days of the charity who had come so far in their recovery that they were now mentoring others. They interviewed women who at times felt they had no hope for a future but who, with the help of the Foundation, had found the self-confidence to get a job or a boyfriend and enjoy life. I had never heard them speak in such a direct way about the difference the Foundation had made to them. When I heard them talk about their break-throughs and achievements, I felt a huge swell of pride for the team who had worked alongside me to make this happen. It was hard to hold back the tears.

By the time the lights came up and Carol Vorderman called me up to join her on stage, the whole room was on their feet. Beyoncé's 'Halo' was playing in the background and I tried to wipe my eyes, and panicked that my nose was running.

'I didn't think I would cry . . .'

Carol held my hand as I thanked Mr Jawad.

'He not only restored me physically through reconstructive surgery, but he believed in me and empowered me to return to work as a professional.'

I looked over at Mum, Dad, Suzy, James and Mr Jawad and could see they all had tears in their eyes as I told the packed room that it wasn't just about me. That I alone wasn't the Katie Piper Foundation; that I was part of a hard-working team who were all devoted to making a difference. And it was true: without the amazing people around me, I wouldn't have achieved half as much.

When I got home I fell into an exhausted sleep with my Pride of Britain Award on my bedside table. The next morning, I was woken up by my ringing phone. I opened my eyes as I reached for the phone, and upon seeing my gleaming award staring back down at me, all the good feelings came flooding back into my system.

I was smiling as I answered. Kay shouted down the line.

'You're mental.'

'Morning, Kay. I was still asleep . . . Why am I mental?'

I sat up in bed, pulling the award onto my lap for a closer look.

'Yesterday, when I asked you what was happening, you said, "not very much".'

'Yeah . . .'

'I read in today's newspaper that you won a bloody Pride of Britain Award! When were you going to tell me?'

'Oh yeah, I was about to get up and start getting ready when you called. I don't know why I didn't mention it . . .'

'It's a Pride . . . of . . . Britain . . . Award.'

'Yup. I'm looking at it right now.'

'Don't move. I'm on my way over. I want to hear all about it.'

I hadn't really told anyone about the award before I actually received it; I had kept it to myself for fear of sounding like I thought I was 'all that'. But I was happy now that my best friend knew. When she got over to my flat that morning we spent hours drinking tea while I told her about every moment of the night before. She asked a million questions and beamed with pride while I marvelled at how lucky I was to have such a selfless friend who'd helped me through every failure and celebrated every success with me.

Chapter Twenty-Two

Just a couple of weeks after Pride of Britain, I was finally on my way up north to film *Secret Millions* at Durham Prison. I'd spent months wrangling over whether to do the show. Even though I had strong views about the men who attacked me, in principle I completely and utterly believed in the premise of the show, which was all about rehabilitation. A shocking 60 per cent of prisoners on a short sentence go on to reoffend within a year of being let out, so anything that might help them give back to society by leading a productive, crime-free life was something I felt I should try to understand as objectively as I could. It was also exactly the sort of show I'd watch if it came on TV. But at the same time, I'd spent years trying to keep myself safe and away from harm, after the brutal crimes I'd suffered, and now here I was, getting ready to walk voluntarily into a building filled with convicted criminals.

The prison was a category B, filled with burglars, people convicted of assault, drug dealers, car thieves, and even murderers. Knowing I'd get an inkling of what life was like for Danny, the man who'd raped me, I couldn't sleep the night before filming started. I was sure it was going to be terrifying, aggressive and oppressive. What if they attacked me? What if they behaved towards me like they did towards Clarice Starling in *Silence Of The Lambs*?

The next morning, exhausted and filled with nerves, my expectations of their living conditions were turned upside down. From an emotional standpoint, I wanted to think of the men who attacked me, and those like them, serving their time in squalid conditions, really being punished for what they did. But in my first few hours behind bars I came to realise this wasn't the case.

Having passed through several huge double-locked doors, we began our tour of the facility. There were games consoles and TVs in some rooms, and each prisoner had their own toilet and freshly laundered clothes. There wasn't a rat, squalid bucket or leaking pipe in sight. The prison library was better stocked than many public libraries; there were even shelves filled with law books. There was a section devoted to books that glamourise crime: Charles Bronson, *Mr Nice*, Costa Del Sol criminals. There was a soft-porn section (well thumbed), poetry section (not so well thumbed), forgiveness section . . . Everything.

Lunch in the canteen was a step up from the school meals I'd had, and some of it looked far nicer than what I usually cooked for myself. It appeared from the outside that, apart from their freedom, everything these prisoners could have wanted was laid on for them.

The opportunities they were given were also very surprising to me. In addition to classes in basic reading and writing skills, computer skills, and the chance to sit GCSEs, many of them had free access to advanced courses, which for anyone in the outside world would cost thousands of pounds.

It all made me feel so conflicted, and I had to work very hard to find a balance between being judgemental and keeping an open mind about each prisoner's circumstances. I felt genuine sympathy for many of them and how hard it was for them to find or be given opportunities that would get them past their crimes once they were released.

A huge proportion of the inmates I spoke to had mental health problems and were suffering from depression too. There were men who were struggling to come off life-long drug dependencies. And the vast majority of them had two things in common: really bad starts in life and periods of homelessness in their adult years. It was pretty heartbreaking to hear many of these stories.

The prison governor explained to me that prison isn't a deterrent for a large proportion of inmates because they have a much better or safer life on the inside than they do on the outside, so they don't fear custodial sentences. For many, a spell behind bars is often preferable to homelessness so they continue reoffending to keep a roof over their heads.

I spoke to an inmate named Neil, who was serving four years for burglary, and what he said backed this up.

'Life's much better in here for me than on the outside. I get my prison skin in here whenever I come back.'

I had no idea what he was talking about.

'What's "prison skin"?' I asked.

'Outside I take drugs, drink too much, sleep rough, have to go out on the rob to get by. Here I get to sleep in a warm clean bed. I can play computer games. I eat three square meals a day; lots of fruit and veg. My skin looks twenty years younger every time I come back. That's my prison skin.'

He wasn't bragging, he was just being honest. Most of us can't comprehend the idea that being locked up might be preferable to life on the outside, but while life stays like that for people like Neil, there's little hope of proper rehabilitation for some career criminals.

Not all the inmates I met thought about prison the way Neil did, and I found myself feeling sorry for a man named Billy who had been in and out of prison for car theft most of his adult life; he'd been brought up by a single mum who'd turned to prostitution when he was a child.

'I fell into robbing when I was a kid,' he told me. 'A bit of me wanted to get out the house and everyone knew Mum was at it. I didn't see any examples in life other than criminals, so I did it too.'

He couldn't hold my gaze for more than a couple of seconds at a time. He tugged constantly at his sleeves, pulling them down over his hands, and had sad, empty eyes. If he'd had any self-confidence when he was first sentenced as a teenager, it had been eroded with every stint he'd done inside.

'I'm nearly thirty-six and I don't feel like a real man. I haven't ever contributed to society. I don't even know how it properly works. I feel useless. I've only ever been a burden.'

He told me he wished he'd done things differently, been someone else. I wondered whether Billy's life had been predetermined for him the minute he was born.

Next I met David, a well-spoken man who had a very different kind of story. A first-time offender at forty-two, he'd been a banker in the City, had gone out one night and got wasted, then driven to work the next morning. There'd been a pile-up he didn't cause but he ended up at the back of the collision. He was breathalysed by the police and found to be over the limit, and was sentenced for dangerous driving while under the influence.

His initial six-month tariff had been increased to three years after a fellow inmate picked a fight with David and he defended himself. Now they each had longer sentences and had lost the right to apply for parole. David had a wife and child who were struggling to get by on the outside without his wages, and he had to accept the fact that he'd never work in the City again. His life would be very different once he was released.

Within a few hours of visiting the prison I realised just how many emotional and social problems a lot of these prisoners had, and how broken, damaged and even vulnerable grown men can be. At times it felt like looking in a mirror, back to where I'd been a few years before, with so many of them voicing feelings that echoed those I'd once had myself. Many had lost hope, had no self-belief and no expectation that life could get any better. They didn't feel capable of digging themselves out of the holes they were in, and held no faith in the fact that they could start functioning once more as useful members of society. None of them believed they would ever matter or make a difference again. I'd felt just like this in the aftermath of my attack.

Even though they were criminals and I was a victim of crime, we had ended up in similar emotional places. We all needed a helping hand up, and a second chance to start living again in a positive, productive way. Spending time with them made me realise that society shouldn't give up on inmates or former inmates just because rehabilitating them seems too challenging. The Acumen Trust was facing an uphill battle to change the viewpoints of employers and local communities, especially during a recession. It was hard not to feel that society had turned on these men. It was too simple an answer just to lump them all together and give them a label of 'bad' or 'useless'; many of the men really did want to turn their lives around but simply didn't know how. They weren't all evil; lots of them were simply damaged.

I started out thinking I wouldn't care for these men. That I *couldn't* care for them because – like the men who attacked me – they had also left victims in their wake. But while some I spoke to showed little genuine remorse, there were others like Billy who did and who in fact, I realised, were also victims themselves.

But despite this, I did struggle to reconcile the fact that it didn't feel like any of them were being punished. I put my issues to the Governor over lunch before I returned to London.

'Like it or not they all have victims, so don't they deserve to be punished for the crimes they committed?'

I didn't see his answer coming, and it touched a nerve.

'Losing your freedom and not getting to see loved ones is the only punishment prison is meant to enforce, and for a lot of the guys in here that's not such a big deal. Prison is meant to be a rehabilitation centre. The courts don't send us monsters just to hurt them and make them bigger monsters and then send them back out into society. That wouldn't help anyone . . .'

He paused before adding,

'Including the victims of their crimes. We're trying to help them become better people than they were when they came in.'

I knew he was right but it was a bitter pill to swallow. Perhaps I would have felt differently if something so awful hadn't happened to me, but it had. I spent the entire train journey back to London replaying what he'd said. The perpetrators of the crime against me *were* monsters, so how would I feel if prison turned them into bigger monsters and *then* they were released? As hard as it was to admit, if and when they do get released, it will be far better if they come out cured, fixed and repentant, and never ever again tempted to visit the kind of hurt they did to me on anyone else.

Chapter Twenty-Three

Filming for *Secret Millions* finished just before Christmas, and with studio voiceovers scheduled for the New Year before the show aired in March 2013, James and I decided we'd spend as much of the festive period together as we could. I gently broke the news to Mum that it would be the first Christmas since my attack that I wouldn't be waking up at our family home.

'Mum, I'm going to stay at James's house on Christmas Eve if that's okay, but I'll come to you first thing Christmas Day. Then can he come and stay at ours on the 27th? I just want to be able to give him his present on Christmas morning in person before I leave.'

'Of course, love. What are you getting him?' She was her usual supportive self.

'A Red Letter Day to drive a sports car round Brands Hatch. It's a surprise; do you think he'll like it?'

'I'm sure he will. Any ideas what he's getting you?'

'Nope, I told him not to spend very much though.'

Waking up next to James on Christmas morning felt like the best start to any Christmas since the attack. He loved his present and when he gave me mine, I spent ages squeezing and shaking it to guess what it was.

'Is it a scarf? A pair of gloves? A tracksuit?' I gave him a cheeky smile.

'Ha ha, very funny. I hope you like it. Go on, open it, Kate.'

'Hang on, I'm enjoying the suspense. Pair of pyjamas?'

'I'll take it back unless you open it *right now*.'

I finally tore off the wrapping and unfolded the most exquisite navy blue Vivienne Westwood dress. Looking from the dress to James, I could barely string my words together.

'Oh my God. I love it. I was looking at this the other day praying it would get reduced in the sales. How did you know? And I told you not to spend too much!'

I was beaming at how thoughtful he was.

'I saw you'd been looking at it on your laptop. I wanted to get you something to show you how much you mean to me.'

I hugged him and kissed his cheek, speechless at his generosity.

'No one's ever bought me clothes before.'

I took the dress with me to my parents' house later that morning to show it off to Mum. I tried it on, and couldn't stop raving about how perfect both it, and James were.

'Can you believe he got the right size and everything?'

I twirled round to show Mum the back. Spinning around again, I caught a shared glance between her and Dad. It was a look I'd last seen at Paul's wedding; their 'everything is going to be alright' look.

The day after going back to work in the New Year, James took me out for dinner.

Since meeting him I'd already changed my hair colour twice, from jet black to dark brown, and then to a softer chestnut colour with caramel highlights. I loved experimenting and had enjoyed all the permutations I'd been through, but because I was feeling so content and confident in all aspects of my life, I started thinking it might be time to go back to blonde and reclaim that part of me. Dying my hair dark had been so symbolic, and it would be just as big a deal going the other way. But this time, it would be for positive reasons.

I put it to James.

'I'm thinking about dying my hair again, what do you reckon?'

He rolled his eyes dramatically.

'How many more colours can you be, Kate?' he teased. 'Since we got together you've been through about four colours and that's just in eight months.'

I laughed with him, but explained further.

'I know, I like switching things up, but I'm thinking of going back to blonde. I dyed my hair originally because I was in a bad place. I didn't want to be seen as a victim any more, by me or anyone else. But now I feel the best I've felt in a very long time and I'm ready to pick up where I left off. Does that make any sense?'

James nodded and smiled, 'It does make sense. And I know it will suit you.'

As 'blonde acid girl' I'd been insecure, lonely, scared and worried about the future. But despite going back to my roots (literally) I knew that scared girl wouldn't be coming back. Besides, with my track record of hairstyles, I could always just change again if I decided to – much to my publishers' exasperation! My good friend and hairdresser Tamie had been the first to colour my hair dark then taking it jet-black for *Things Get Better*.

I was excited about being blonde again but in the run-up to the appointment it dawned on me that changing my hair was nothing compared with all the other things about me that had changed. Before the attack I'd been image-obsessed, always wanting to look perfect and pretty. Now I cared about much bigger things in my life than simply how I looked: my family, my health, my relationships.

I also realised that, since the attack, constantly changing my hair had become a form of expressing myself. Because my face is made up from grafted skin, which doesn't move in the same way as normal facial skin, I have a limited range of facial expressions. So hair, make-up and fashion are all ways in which I'm able to express my emotions on the outside.

My good friend and London-based hairdresser Mikey came over and took me back to blonde again. Once he'd finished, we hugged. He had been through all my identity changes with me and he knew this was important to me. I felt like the final bits of the puzzle were falling into place. Now, in January 2013, as a new year was beginning, being Katie didn't feel scary any more, and because James accepted me, I found it easier to accept myself, to be me again.

A month later, Scar Academy was finally held at St Bart's Hospital in London after so much hard work and planning. This two-day conference was one of the most significant events we'd ever been involved in, and in the end it was attended by sixty-eight representatives, including ones from every hospital with burns facilities in the UK, academics, doctors, nurses, occupational therapists and physiotherapists; people attended from every level of care.

We also invited a range of experts in very specific fields, including burns and plastic surgeons, professors in skin regeneration and wound healing, and research fellows from centres across Europe, including the one in France where I'd had my rehabilitation, to share their knowledge. There were lectures, discussions and workshops, covering everything to do with burns and scars. I also gave a talk, as did Mr Jawad, as a trustee of the Foundation and the surgeon who'd saved my life after the attack and given me hope ever since. There was also a hair-transplant expert, and skin-camouflage practitioners, who specialise in covering scars. For many burns survivors, this element of burns recovery is just as important as the medical side, so it was vital to include it alongside the science.

Many of the people who worked so hard to take Scar Academy from dream to reality were in fact people whom the Foundation had helped over the last four years. Our volunteers were there in force over the two days too, welcoming registrants, helping to analyse data for presentations, and participating in practical demonstrations. It was a real team effort. The survivors who helped were shining examples of our vision as a charity – men and women who existed in a world where scars do not limit their function, social inclusion or sense of wellbeing. So all the people who attended arrived to witness burns survivors in front-facing public roles, positions of responsibility. Their presence and efforts made a strong statement.

Long-term, the Foundation's main desire is to see an increase in effective treatment options available to patients in the UK, because where there are options, there is hope. Statistics show that every year in the UK approximately 250,000 people suffer a burn injury, of which 175,000 go to A&E and 13,000 are admitted to hospital. Scar Academy UK allowed the Foundation to share knowledge about some of the beneficial treatments I received in France, and others that we've been investigating, which aren't routinely available here.

Before it had even finished we knew Scar Academy had been a roaring success. Walking through the conference hall, I caught snapshots of conversations and saw people interacting with one another exactly as we had hoped they would. Me, my Foundation colleagues and all the people who collaborated with us from Oscare and Queen Mary University could see that there was a good atmosphere at the event, and we all felt encouraged that these conversations might continue long afterwards. Seeing it all go off without a hitch made me feel so proud of what has been achieved since those early days, back when the Foundation consisted of just me, alone in my bedroom on a laptop. I am so pleased that the Foundation is now firmly established and that we're able to offer help and support to the many who need it, both in our daily work and in collaboration with so many incredible supporters and specialists.

Chapter Twenty-Four

Once Scar Academy was over, I finally had time to catch up on other things. My flat was at last on the market, and with lots of viewings and assurances from my estate agent that it would sell quickly, James and I now stepped up the search for our new home, spending hours trawling online property sites and viewing several houses every weekend.

Despite endless hunting, nothing had yet ticked all our boxes. I wanted security; he wanted a big garden. I wanted a walk-in wardrobe; he wanted the potential for a loft conversion further down the line. Finally, after months of searching, we found the one. It had the lot. As we walked round our dream home, we exchanged excited glances and squeezed one another's hand. It was perfect. When our offer was accepted I was elated.

I joked with James. 'God, I'm not sure I can cope with an actual move now, I'm knackered!'

'Ha, don't worry,' he assured me. 'I'll help you pack up. I'll rope in a mate, too, so if you want to be foreman you can tell us what to pack where and we'll get it all done for you.'

In order to get ahead and make things easier for James on moving day, I dismantled every piece of flat-pack furniture so that it was ready to be taken away. But in what can at best be described as sheer disorganisation and at worst as complete stupidity, I got my dates mixed up with all the paperwork flying between solicitors and spent the final fortnight in my disassembled flat sleeping on the floor. Genius!

With an aching back come moving day, James and his friend Stu ferried boxes from my front door down to their waiting vans. As they worked, and I watched my little flat empty out, I smiled as I thought about how far I'd come, and how different I felt to the girl who'd first moved in – even though I'd started and ended my time there sleeping on the floor.

A stirring behind me brought me out of my thoughts and back to the job in hand.

'Err, Kate, what's all this, hmm?'

Spinning on my heels, I saw that James had pulled up a rug I'd put down before he came over for the very first time. While it didn't cover every sin and spill on the carpet, it did cover a huge fake-tan stain, which had grown bigger during the four years I lived there. He stood there pointing at the splodge, tapping his foot.

'Oh, I didn't think you'd notice,' I said sheepishly.

'Kate, it'd be impossible not to notice. I also noticed how it's spattered all over the rest of the carpet too. How can someone miss their legs so much? Or were you intending to tan the carpet?'

I put my hands on my hips, feigning indignation.

'Very funny. You wouldn't understand.'

James got on his hands and knees and started rolling up the rug while I continued to defend myself.

'See, if I'd stopped to wipe it up I'd have ended up with blotchy patches, where one bit dried before the rest. You have to apply evenly.'

'So you decided to let the carpet get blotchy instead?'

'Kind of . . .'

He got to his feet.

'Right: rule number one in our new house is no fake tanning unless it's in the shower, and you have to wipe down the tiles afterwards. Or you can do it in the utility room and clean up after yourself.'

He hoisted the rug onto his shoulder, giving me a wink before he started off down the stairs. I stood there smiling. The only words I had heard were 'Our New House'. It had a nice ring to it.

Later that day, after several long, tiring hours getting our stuff into our new home, Stu left and James and I ordered a take-away before collapsing into bed. Thankfully we'd managed to find the box with the sheets, and despite the fact that the rest of the house looked like a tip, with up-ended furniture, lamps plugged in without their shades, and half-unpacked boxes all over the place, we were both excited at finally sleeping in our own bed, in our own home. Together.

As we began the task of finding homes for our stuff over the next few days, I found a box of his photos. It gave me an idea. Putting the lid straight back on the box, I jumped up and announced that we were going out. With the box under my arm, I headed downstairs.

'Kate,' he protested. 'We've still got tons to do.'

'Don't worry, it'll all still be here when we get back.'

He followed me downstairs, looking bemused.

'What are you up to, Kate?'

I stopped and looked him in the eye.

'James, I want this place to be ours, properly ours. Have you seen how many pictures and memories I have up around us already? Loads. Have you seen how many you've got? None. I want your pictures here too.'

I handed him the box.

'I want us to have a house filled with both our memories. And I want us to build new ones together.'

He took the box from me, smiling and knowing I wouldn't be dissuaded. Three hours later we returned home with photos of his childhood, family and friends, reprinted and framed. Together, we hung them on the walls.

We'd done as a couple what I'd spent weeks doing on my own when I'd first moved into my flat. We were now surrounded by pictures of the people who'd helped each of us get to where we were, and who would continue to do so now we were together. Seeing our photos mingling on the same wall cemented the fact that we were building a life together. I now had a partner beside me on my life's path, the one I'd walked alone for the last five years.

The following morning James caught me putting on my make-up, even though all we were doing was staying in and unpacking. It was still a big deal for me if he saw me without make-up, so I avoided it as much as possible, even though I was confident he loved me however I looked. I was mid-mascara when I felt his arms encircle my waist.

'We're not going out, are we?'

'No, I just . . .'

He looked at me, puzzled.

'Just what?'

I trailed off. I could feel my back getting clammy. His arms were still around my waist and we were staring at our reflection in the mirror together. He turned me round to face him. Looking me square in the eyes, he spoke.

'Kate, you know it's okay to be you. I'll always fancy you. I'll always love you. We're soul mates and I'll never ever leave you. I won't ever feel sorry for you. I won't ever pity you. I love you whether you have make-up on or you're dribbling in your sleep.'

I could feel tears pricking my eyes, spilling over before I had a chance to get a tissue. I turned back to face the mirror.

'Now look what you've done, you've made my mascara run . . .'

We laughed as I sniffed.

He kissed my shoulder and headed downstairs while I scraped back my hair and reached for my wipes to take off my make-up. James loved me. Proper love. Unconditional love. Not love with an agenda. He loved and accepted me for me.

Kay had sent us a housewarming card shortly after we moved in and wanted to come and visit the new Casa Piper, but now it was March and her baby was nearly a fortnight overdue.

I was checking in on her every day to see if there'd been any movement. I called her early one Sunday while James was still asleep.

'So, anything yet?'

She sounded fed up of waiting.

'Nope, still nothing. I really want to meet this baby, Kate. I feel like I've been pregnant forever.'

'It'll happen soon, honestly. Call me if you need me and I'll check in on you tomorrow.'

Later that evening, I was clearing up after dinner when her name flashed up on my phone. It was a text.

'I'VE HAD MY BABY BOY!!!!!!!!'

I almost dropped the saucepan and called through to James in the next room.

'Oh my God, James! Kay's had her baby. I just spoke to her this morning and she was complaining about being overdue. I can't believe he's here; it must have happened so fast. I have to go and see her.'

I jumped up and down and gave him a big hug before grabbing my shoes and sprinting to the car. I drove as fast as I legally could to the hospital.

Not wanting to turn up empty-handed, I stopped on the way to pick up a card and some small presents. Kay had given birth in Tooting, at the same hospital I had visited every four weeks back when I had my plastic scar compression masks. I knew exactly where the car park and the entrance were, so I ditched the car and dashed in. I found the ward and as I tried to catch my breath one of the midwives told me that Kay had been lucky enough to get a private room because the ward was so quiet that evening. She pointed me down the hallway. I took a deep breath and knocked on the door.

'Hey, Mum, how are you?'

'Kate! Come in, he's sleeping.'

I hadn't taken two steps into the room when I started to cry. I peered over at her tiny little boy.

'Look at him,' I said. 'He's perfect. You're perfect.'

Kay's boyfriend Ivan was standing protectively over his fiancée and new son. He gave me a kiss and said he was going out for a minute to get something to eat. Kay smiled at my tears.

'Kate, why are you crying, you loon?'

'You all look so beautiful, so happy, so complete.' I said, through my sniffles. 'You look knackered though,' I teased.

She shot me a look and we both smiled.

'So would you in my position, Tiny!'

'Have you decided on a name?' I asked.

She turned him towards me. 'This is Noah James. You want to hold him?'

I couldn't believe she was offering.

'Can I? I'm a bit scared. I don't know what to do.'

Kay placed Noah gently in my arms and I watched him sleep. I was so thrilled for my best friend.

When I got home a few hours later, I couldn't stop talking about the baby.

'James, Noah is so amazing, I can't wait for you to meet him. He's a proper little person. They're a family, the three of them. Kay and Ivan are Mummy and Daddy now. Isn't it incredible? Imagine being bound like that by shared love for someone else.'

James's next words gave me a heart-quickening jolt.

'Well we're bound together forever aren't we? It's just at the moment our love isn't shared with a baby. It will be one day though.'

During our time together we'd talked vaguely about the fact we each saw children as part of our lives down the line, and I had told him about my adoption plans. But suddenly the conversation wasn't so vague.

'Do you really think we'll be parents one day?'

James held my face and looked intently into my eyes.

'I know we'll be parents one day. It's just a matter of time. Kate, look at us. We've got a house big enough for a family, we've both got good jobs, we're both thirty this year. Isn't it a question of "when", not "if"?'

That night we decided we'd start trying for a family of our own in the summer.

Although James loved the idea of adopting and agreed it would be an amazing thing to do one day, we decided to try for our own baby first, even though we knew that the anti-rejection drugs I had taken might have affected my fertility. We talked into the small hours about what kind of parents we wanted to be, what names we liked, how we wanted to raise our kids, and who we wanted as potential godparents. Of course, I had to call Kay immediately to tell her our plans – she'd been involved in so many decisions I'd made in my life, and she and her beautiful baby had kick-started the conversation for this new one too!

Here was the start of another new chapter in my life, and the furthest into the future that I'd dared to look since the attack. I saw James and me, living our lives, raising a family and growing old, together, and it was wonderful.

Chapter Twenty-Five

Over the next few weeks I spent as much time as I could with Kay and Noah, but I was also in overdrive again at work, sorting the final few tables for the Foundation's annual fundraising ball and auction. We'd raised over £200,000 at the previous one and we were desperate to do just as well with this one, if not better.

Many celebrity guests were confirmed as coming, including Caroline Flack, Dionne Bromfield, Sarah Harding, Alex Jones, Lydia Bright, Danielle O'Hara, Louie Spence, Barbara Windsor, Nick Knowles, Brooke Kinsella and Tamara Ecclestone, to name just a few. And, of course, our patron, Simon Cowell.

I'd arranged to get ready at the hotel right after helping to make sure the banquet room looked perfect. The team from the Foundation had worked tirelessly for hours to get everything ready to go – from preparing goody bags full of amazing donated gifts to the hand-written place cards at every seat – and as I went upstairs to change into my dress they were still perfecting a few finishing touches. I tried to relax while I got ready, but nerves were starting to get the better of me. I knew we'd all done everything we could to make the night run smoothly but I wanted everyone to have a good time, and I knew that this, in turn, would mean more money for the Foundation.

The guests arrived, all looking glam in their finest black tie and gowns, and the evening began. Adrenaline was pumping as the auction approached, but Simon helped calm my nerves.

'Katie, you look fantastic.'

He squeezed my hand before walking out on stage to kick off proceedings, and he did so with a bang.

'Right now, before we even start, I'm donating £10,000 to the Katie Piper Foundation, just for holding this event and inviting us all to such a great evening. Who's going to beat me and donate more than £10,000?'

He turned to me with a wink and flashed his perfect smile. I loved that he started the auction by auctioning nothing more than the chance to outbid him – even though no one took him up on it!

But even so, after that we were off. Barbara Windsor bid thousands of pounds for a set of One Direction concert tickets, which I later learned she gave to a children's charity to auction off again. She's one of the most selfless women I've ever met; down to earth, warm and incredibly passionate, and extremely eloquent about good causes.

Tamara Ecclestone bid on every single thing that came up just to get the bids to go higher. She spent thousands on a Holmes Place gym membership – admitting when I asked her afterwards that she had her own private gym in her London home. It was so funny, and I loved that she was so enthusiastic and supportive. It was completely in the spirit of the evening. Tamara's donated at every ball since I started the Foundation and does everything she can to help out and be proactive. When people criticise her in the press it's so unfair – I know what a big, generous heart she really has.

Jahméne Douglas, who'd been a finalist on *The X Factor*, not only bid like crazy at the auction but also provided the entertainment for the night, and brought the house down. Jahméne is close to the charity because when he was a child his mum was violently abused and burned by his father. I'm very fond of both Jahméne and his mum.

As I said the final goodbyes at the end of the night and we gave out the goody bags, I knew everyone who attended would remember the night forever. I was staggered the following week when we did the final sums and learned we'd raised more than double what we could have hoped for. It was going to make such a difference to what we could do at the Foundation, and was a testament to all the hard work of the staff and board of trustees. I'm always amazed at how much passion and care they put into what they do.

Despite having planned some down-time after the event, the following week I received an exciting call from my agent. She told me the *Daily Mirror* wanted me to write one of their columns for a few weeks. On top of that, they also wanted me to be a judge for this year's Pride of Britain Awards.

On hearing this news, I got butterflies in my tummy. I coughed, trying to compose myself. I was sure I'd heard her wrong, but before I could reply, Joanne said, 'You'd be a perfect judge, Katie. Your award last year proves that. Your work really makes a difference to a lot of people and you know what being a fighter and achieving against the odds is all about. You'll do a great job.'

I accepted without hesitation.

A few days later I received a huge file of nominations. There were twelve categories, with five nominations in each. That meant sixty life stories, achievements and accomplishments to familiarise myself with, and I wanted to make sure I got to grips with every person's entry well in advance of the day of judging, which was due to take place in a few weeks.

About the same time, I was asked to go on a remarkable mission to Tanzania for a week with a team of doctors and nurses from the Northern Burn Care Unit in Northumberland, where I'd been to visit some burn survivors a few months before. They work in partnership with the Kilimanjaro Christian Medical Centre who, among many other things, take burns medics out to Tanzania to help with operations. They educate local doctors and nurses about immediate care to minimise the impact of burns, and they teach them about long-term scar management.

After my visit to the patients in Northumberland they had asked me if I'd be willing to accompany them to Tanzania as an educational speaker on their next annual visit. They wanted me to go along as a burns survivor who could empathise with the patients' experiences and to help to educate the locals and medical staff about patient, and integration back into the community.

I'd been asked on trips overseas before but had had to turn the requests down, as I hadn't wanted to just 'go and look' without making a difference. So the opportunity to counsel local patients and talk to their families about disfigurement, life after burns and reintegration back into their tribal communities after injury made it feel like a truly worthwhile and giving experience. So when the call came saying they were planning their trip, I felt I was able to contribute something and should go. It was my first foreign trip to meet fellow burns survivors who were coping in the developing world, and I was both excited and nervous.

The time came for my trip and while I packed my suitcase, I chatted to James, telling him excitedly about the challenges I was expecting to face in Tanzania and about the amazing stories I was reading in the Pride of Britain nominations. But as I threw things into my bag, James's mind was elsewhere.

'Kate, promise me that once you're home from your trip you'll take it a bit easier? You've been working way too hard. It wouldn't hurt to take your foot off the gas a bit.'

He was worried about me. Not to mention the fact that though we'd started trying for a baby a few weeks before, finding the time together wasn't easy with our crazy schedules.

I knew he was right.

'I promise. We always knew these few months were going to be busy.'

I had a packed schedule in Tanzania; I visited schools, churches, hospitals, orphanages and communities. I loved being there and would definitely go back, but it was like nothing I'd ever seen or experienced before. Burns are a huge problem for the twelve-million-strong population who are serviced by just one specialist medical centre, and while the staff there see thousands of burns victims every year, there are many more who simply don't make it that far. Electricity in outer lying villages is patchy at best, and when it fails, families often cook on kerosene campfires. Children often crawl or fall into the fires, or the fires set light to mosquito nets while families are asleep. The local community is told about the visiting medical team months in advance and so people come from miles around to be seen by the Western doctors who have exceptional experience with burns and scars.

On our first day there I met a boy named Jonah. He was eight years old and had fallen onto a kerosene lantern three years before and burned his arms and trunk. The tops of his arms had welded to his body as he recovered and he'd been left unable to use or move his arms above the elbow. The scars on his hands had retracted and with no release operations he couldn't close his fists or work his fingers. He was a football-mad little boy with a huge smile and a fantastic sense of humour who couldn't pick up or throw a ball.

I also met Peter. He was fifteen and, incredibly, had walked for two days to be seen by the medics at the centre. He had burns over his face, neck and body from a kerosene accident years before. Because his scars had retracted, he was living in constant pain, with no access to pain relief unless he walked nearly thirty miles to get it.

Thankfully, both Jonah and Peter would now get the prescription medication and surgery they needed, but I couldn't help but wonder how many more children there were just like them who hadn't come to the hospital.

I've always been grateful for the exceptional treatment I received both from the NHS and in France – it literally saved my life and rebuilt both my body and my mind. The children and adults I met in Tanzania are not so fortunate and more often than not have no choice but to adapt to their disfigurements, live with unnecessary pain, and face social exclusion in a way no one should. It's a problem that can't be fixed overnight but little by little the medical team out there and visiting teams like ours are making a difference. But there is so much more yet that still needs to be done and despite how many people they helped, I knew it was only the tip of the iceberg. Having just one medical centre to serve twelve million people is like trying to row across an ocean in a paper boat. It's simply not enough to deliver the kind of care, both immediate and ongoing, that is desperately needed out there.

By the end of each day, I found myself completely exhausted, emotionally as well as physically. I put it down to jetlag, the basic accommodation, and the fact that I was finding it hard to sleep. The restless nights made it a struggle to get up in the mornings. I also wasn't eating all that much; I just didn't have much of an appetite. Little did I know I was already pregnant. I tried to unwind in the evenings with my fellow travellers, hoping that time would get me ready to sleep – I even had a puff or two on a cigarette to try to relax me, which I never would have done had I known what was really going on inside me!

After an exhausting week, we boarded the plane back to the UK. During the flight I mused on the longer-term plans for my Foundation. Wondering whether – with enough time and money – some day we could be part of the solution for burns in the developing world as well as in the UK. But for the time being, as I was just about to find out, I was going to have a lot more in my own life to think about.

Fabulous

THE INSPIRATION ISSUE

Photographed
exclusively
for Fabulous by
David Bailey

S&Mpowering
Career advice,
Christian Grey style

Junior Senior
Rock A/W whatever
your age

'I FEEL BLESSED'

In her first interview
since announcing her
pregnancy, **Katie Piper**
on never giving up
on happiness

David Bailey's portrait of me: being shot by such a famous and influential
photographer was an amazing experience.

I was six months pregnant here, giving a speech for the Katie Piper Foundation. Talking one-on-one about my experiences can still be difficult, but sharing my story with a room full of people helps me feel in control and gives me a real sense of achievement.

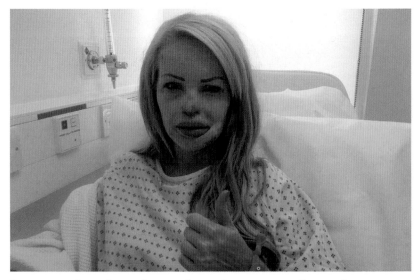

Recovering after a skin graft to my chin and nose – in an effort to release contracted scar tissue.

This was taken at the Oxford Union, after I spoke to the students there. It was quite intimidating to speak at such a prestigious venue, but the experience ended up being incredibly poignant and rewarding.

With my amazing dad at the Chelsea Flower Show. Moving out of my parents' house after the attack was a big step: no one has been more important to my recovery than they have.

At home one Christmas with my ever-faithful dog Barclay. He was a huge part of my recovery team after the attack, and I miss him constantly.

Me and my bump! This was taken just before an appearance on *Loose Women* to talk about my pregnancy – check out the 'yummy mummy' mug they gave me!

Now with an even bigger bump, at a photoshoot for Kiddicare. Work kept me busy throughout my pregnancy…

…but I also found lots of time to get ready for our little girl's arrival.

Belle Elizabeth, born on the 14th of March 2014.
She's my Beautiful Ever After!

Chapter Twenty-Six

I'd been back from Tanzania for a few weeks when I noticed my period was a couple of days late. While I'd never have dared say so out loud, I dreamt it might be because I was pregnant. I happened to have some cheap pregnancy tests at home that I'd bought on a whim from the Pound Shop before my trip, figuring I might need them eventually. So when I was late, curiosity got the better of me and I decided to have a go, literally.

Having done the deed, I put the lid on the stick and washed my hands. The leaflet said to wait three minutes but after counting a minute and a half in my head I swore I could see a line start to appear in the tiny window. I thought I must be imagining things.

I checked the instructions on the box over and over. A line meant the test had worked, two lines meant I was pregnant. But the blue lines were incredibly faint and because I was staring at them constantly I couldn't tell for sure whether they were getting darker and whether there were actually two of them! Resting the test on the closed toilet seat, I washed my hands again, closing my eyes for the final forty-five seconds of the countdown. When I opened my eyes, my heart somersaulted in my chest. There were definitely two dark blue lines. According to my Pound Shop pregnancy test, I was having a baby.

In a state of utter shock, I took a deep breath and swallowed hard before I unlocked the door and prepared to tell James. I wandered tentatively into the kitchen where he was making dinner. My tummy was filled with butterflies, my hands were clammy and I could hear my heart beating in my ears. I could feel the adrenaline start to rise from the pit of my stomach.

It was all so sudden and so overwhelming. I'd have bet the house it would take us well over a year to conceive, and that was if we were lucky. We were only just starting to take it more seriously now that I was home.

I stood for ages before I said anything, watching James's strong back as he stood at the stove. Finally I found the words.

'James, guess what? I think I'm pregnant.'

'Ha ha, very funny.' He just kept stirring the pasta and didn't look up.

I stayed silent. He finally stopped stirring and turned towards me. My expression and the pregnancy test I was holding out assured him I wasn't joking. I searched his face for a reaction but I could see him searching mine too. Neither of us knew how to respond. Now that we were faced with the real possibility we were bringing a new life into the world, the enormity of the situation engulfed us both. It wasn't like in the movies when everyone jumps around with elation and confident delight, kissing each other and making joyous phone calls to family. Instead, our eyes locked, each hoping for some hint of what to do next. In a flash, everything had changed and yet stayed oddly the same. The pasta was still on the stove, the washing still had to come out of the machine and the lounge still needed to be hoovered.

Should we call our parents? The doctor? The *One Born Every Minute* team? I finally found my voice.

'What do we do now?'

James was still at a loss for words. The best he could offer was, 'I don't know'.

Enter Google, stage left. A quick check on the NHS Direct website and ten minutes later we were on our way to Sainsbury's to get a more accurate digital test to figure out just how pregnant I was.

As we got out of the car I said to James, 'You go and get it, I don't want anyone to recognise me. I'll be over by the magazines. Make sure you get the right test.'

I was completely flustered. I tried to look nonchalant and relaxed while I pretended to flip through *Grazia*, but with hindsight I probably just looked like a dodgy shoplifter. I couldn't keep still, fidgeting and peering over my shades to make sure no one was watching me, pulling up the collar of my trench coat like I was Mrs Columbo. I jumped and let out a little yelp when James approached me clutching the shopping bag. We both darted back to the car, and the minute we reached the house I sprinted through the front door and up the stairs before he'd even turned off the car engine.

Those next three minutes were the longest of my life. The test showed I was more than three weeks pregnant but how much more was anyone's guess. I hadn't kept track of my cycle very well. I went back through my diaries, trying my best to remember when my last period had been, and plugged my best estimation of the dates into the NHS Online due date calendar. I clicked on 'go', waiting for my laptop to show me the date on which my baby would come into the world.

The date that popped up was Thursday, 27 March 2014. I was stunned. This was the date of the six-year anniversary of when I was raped. My life had changed irrevocably on that date and it looked likely that it would do exactly the same thing again. I felt sick at the thought of it. For five years that date had been such a dark day for me. I never knew what to do on it when it came round each year; it's not exactly an anniversary to be celebrated, but ignoring it always seemed to underplay its significance. I didn't tell James straight away, I just kept replaying the date in my head, trying to adjust my mindset about what was on the screen in front of me.

Maybe this was meant to be; a joyous celebration to replace a mournful anniversary. The 27 March would no longer be about what I lost in 2008. It would be about what I gained in 2014. Years from now, I'd organise birthday parties with balloons, presents, cake, happiness, joy. All the love that would surround that date would forevermore block out the bleak darkness that had previously owned it. From now on, that date would fill my heart with love and make me smile.

I then counted back to see the actual date I'd conceived. It turned out to be 22 June 2013. My stomach lurched and I started panicking. I'd been in Tanzania less than two weeks afterwards. My mind raced. I'd taken a long-haul flight to get there, had a couple of puffs on a ciggie in the evenings, and hygiene there wasn't up to the standards I was used to. With little refrigeration, meat was left out before being cooked, not something we ever do here. Had I put my baby at risk? What if I'd harmed him or her somehow? I kept touching and staring at my flat tummy, unable to fathom what was going on inside me, but petrified I'd already jeopardised my baby's precious future.

James and I spent the rest of the night on our laptops reading everything we could, with me trying to angle my screen away from him to see whether I'd harmed our baby, our miracle child. After all, when women try for a baby they're supposed to take supplements, improve their diet, avoid alcohol. I hadn't yet begun any of that. Instead I'd been in the slums, eating food that hadn't agreed with me.

Exhausted after reading entirely too many opinions on Netmums, we went to bed and cuddled, each of us clinging to the other. But as James slept, I stared at his silhouette in the dark, wondering what was going on in his mind and praying everything would be okay with our unborn child. We woke the following morning to find both his and my hands resting protectively on my tummy.

By the time we got home from work that evening, we'd each already spent hours on our own thinking about the pregnancy, but the atmosphere wasn't any less loaded. He headed out and went to the gym until 10pm and I sat at home wondering what the hell had happened to my secure, solid, 'can-tell-each-other-anything' relationship. But his time spent bench pressing and my time alone in the house proved to be the space we both needed. When he came in, neither of us said anything about the previous twenty-four hours, but he collapsed in a heap next to me on the sofa, laying his head on my shoulder, and we both started talking about the life we were bringing into his world together. It was then I think we realised we both felt exactly the same: scared, vulnerable, worried, responsible and anxious. But it was a lot more reassuring to feel all those things *together* than it had been to feel them alone. We didn't need to explain or excuse our reactions; we were bound by love and now we were bound as a family. It had just been an overwhelming shock that we weren't expecting, and we had simply needed to let it all sink in.

From then on, it was smooth sailing and we sat there that night talking about what our life would be like as a family, the three of us. It was a reminder that things don't always happen how you plan, and that curve balls – including good ones – can come from anywhere to change things in a way you could never have seen coming.

Those little blue lines, that promise of another new beginning, reaffirmed my feeling that we all have a plan in life that's written for us. This is the only way I've ever been able to make any sense of anything that's happened in my life. I learned the hard way in my mid-twenties that you simply can't control everything that happens to you, and you have to accept that some of it just won't make sense. If you question why things happen or try to change the things you can't, you'll tie yourself in knots looking for answers you may never find, and you may miss out on the good things and new opportunities that might be right in front of you.

I started to think that my surprise baby must be the 'smooth' that was sent to countenance the 'rough' I'd put up with for years. The brightness to balance out the dark from which I'd emerged. It was clearly my destiny to become a mother at thirty, and I couldn't wait.

Chapter Twenty-Seven

When James and I visited the GP a few days later we learned I was six weeks' pregnant and so still roughly still six weeks away from my first NHS scan. We decided to keep things quiet within our inner circle for the time being while we continued to get our heads around our news, but we were too excited to keep it from our parents until we reached the magic twelve-week milestone, when the risk of miscarriage reduces. I always want to share good things with Mum and Dad as soon as they happen, to let them enjoy the positives and try to make up for some of the hurt they've endured on their journey with me. After all, they were the ones who sat outside the operating theatre for over seven hours right after my attack, not knowing whether I'd live or die, as damaged and burned muscle tissue was taken from my corroding face. They were the ones who held me through countless night terrors and flashbacks when I was sure the men who hurt me had escaped from prison and were in my bedroom.

They had spent months holding my hands, walking on either side of me (as they promised they would), when they coaxed me out of the house for longer and longer walks with Barclay during my recovery. They never faltered, never angered, never gave me anything other than love, devotion, time and confidence. So of course I wanted to share with them as soon as possible the news of their first grandchild. But strangely, telling my parents was far more stressful than it had been telling James. I'd just blurted it out to him in mild hysteria, but I wanted to make sure I told my parents in the best way I possibly could.

I knew I couldn't tell them on the phone; I wanted to see their faces so they couldn't hide how they felt. James and I had wondered if we should get married when we started trying but had decided we already knew we would spend the rest of our lives together. Our love was binding enough, a marriage certificate could wait. We were both fine doing things the other way round, but what if my parents didn't understand? What if they were disappointed we'd only been together fourteen months instead of saving marriage and children until we had been in a steady seven-year relationship? I felt like I was sixteen years old and going home to tell my parents I had done something naughty, not that I was nearly thirty and making informed adult decisions. It was hard not to see the funny side.

I called Mum and asked if they wanted to meet in Richmond for Sunday lunch. We'd seen them only the weekend before, so Mum was slightly suspicious as to why I was desperate to meet up two consecutive weekends on the trot.

'But we only just saw you both, Kate.'

'We don't need an excuse or schedule to meet, do we? We'll see you and Dad in Richmond.'

I hung up before she could back out.

Sunday was a warm, sunny day, the kind of day that puts a smile on your face no matter what your mood. I picked out a white embroidered sundress and paired it with some gold gladiator sandals. Checking my reflection in the mirror, I thought it straddled the line between young and carefree, yet responsible and mature. But while my clothes may have been the perfect 'let's tell the parents' outfit, the whole drive there saw me veering between excitement and nerves, not to mention a hearty dose of nausea – a mixture of morning sickness and worry at the thought of them being disappointed in me. That fear made me more nervous about telling them than I'd felt about some of the operations I'd been through. Given the choice, I'd happily have opted for a general anaesthetic for a few hours rather than having to deliver the news that I was carrying their first grandchild.

I had no idea exactly how to do it, either – should it be a big drum-roll moment or should I just let it slip out like it was no big deal? Would I look them both in the eye, or just Mum? Would I be able to tell them without crying? Should James and I hold hands and deliver the news together? Or would it be better if he delivered the news while I beamed in the background, implying we were both in control and had longed for this moment? It seemed such a huge piece of news to drop on them. We'd all remember this day forever, and one day they'd tell our child about the day they learnt they would become Grandma and Grandpa. The pressure to get it right, to make it perfect, was huge.

We'd arranged to meet at one of our favourite restaurants. We arrived and weaved through the tables to where they were already waiting. After hugging them both, we sat down and I opened my mouth to tell them straight away.

'Mum . . .'

A voice behind me interrupted.

'Hello everybody, can I get you some drinks while you have a look at the menu?'

I was milliseconds from blurting out to our waiter that I was pregnant! We ordered drinks and I hid behind the menu, catching my breath.

'What were you going to say, Kate?' Mum asked.

'Oh, nothing. I like your top.'

We ate our meal while I made small talk and said nothing. By the time dessert came and then coffee, James was convinced I'd chickened out of telling them and was gently nudging me under the table. I was aching to get the words out but the place was packed and I was paranoid. People sometimes tweet me when I'm out to say, 'I'm sat near you,' so the last thing I wanted that day was to tell Mum and have someone on the next table tweet me congratulations, having overheard my intensely private news.

By the time the bill came, it was clear I wasn't going to tell them there. I knew Mum would react – maybe throwing her hands up in joy or disbelief – so there was a distinct possibility that telling them would draw unwanted attention. I suggested we take a walk down the river so I could tell them in the quiet, private sunshine on the banks of the Thames. As we strolled along, I opened my mouth a million times and took a deep breath but the words wouldn't come. Before I knew it, we were at the end of the river walk, with nothing but sandbags in front of us.

They knew something was up as we turned around to walk right back the way we had come. With my mounting tension weighing down the atmosphere, I cleared my throat and finally opened my mouth.

'Yeah, so, ahh, right, there is a reason I asked you to come to lunch today.'

They exchanged a look I'd seen pass between them a thousand times. It was their 'Oh-no-what's-Kate-done-or-planning-now?' look.

'It's because you're going to be grandparents.'

Mum's mouth hung open. Dad looked at her and he spoke first. 'I told you!'

His face had lit up into a big smile and he was now switching his eyes between James and me, trying to read how we were feeling about it.

'We thought it was weird you wanted to meet up two weekends running, I told your mum it was either because you were getting married or that you were having a baby.'

He looked like he'd just answered the $64,000 question.

'Are you planning to get married then?' he continued.

'Dad!'

James leapt in to save my blushes. 'I'm working on it,' he promised, surprising me and delighting Dad in equal measure.

Mum was starting to digest our news. They both asked James if he was happy, and when he assured them he was over the moon and they could see we were both delighted, they visibly relaxed and couldn't stop smiling. We walked back along the river together, but like a child with a school report, I had to keep checking they were happy, that they were still proud of me and I hadn't let them down.

'You think it's good news, then?' I asked Mum.

'Yes, darling. Just think, it'll be the first time since you were born you'll be in and out of hospital for something good rather than something bad.'

They knew how much this baby defied the odds. For them, like me, it was a resounding reminder that I'd survived.

We sat down for ice cream and it seemed like everyone who walked past us was pregnant or pushing a pram.

Dad said, 'I can't believe I'm going to be a grandpa.'

Mum chimed in, 'I want to be called Grandma, not Granny.'

I was euphoric – and very relieved.

Of course, my parents were only one part of the equation, we also had to tell James's. We went straight over to see them that same day to give them our news. Even though we'd just got it all out with my parents, it was just as nerve-wracking to do it all over again with his. James and I sat with them on the sofa for ages, watching TV and nudging each other – James thought I should tell them, but I thought he should break the ice. Finally James gave in and cleared his throat.

'Katie's got something to tell you,' he said.

I tried to subtly elbow him, but there was no going back and together we shared our news. They were so excited, and just like my parents, they admitted they knew something was up when we called to say we were coming over. I swear they all must have had some kind of grandchild radar! Our baby would be their fourth grandchild, James's brother has two children and his sister has one, but they were just as excited as my parents had been for their first.

With both sets of parents duly ticked off the 'let's tell' list, next was Suzy. I promised Mum and Dad I'd tell her when she came to stay with me the following weekend.

It was all part of an elaborate plan I was concocting. When the GP had told us we'd have to wait six weeks for our scan, we looked into getting a private scan from our local hospital, just to make sure everything was all right. I booked one for the Saturday Suzy was coming and then let James in on the plot.

'I'll tell her right when she comes on Friday night, then we can all go to the scan together on Saturday. Then when we Skype Paul and Leah that night, I can show them the scan.'

He agreed it was a great way to let them all know.

I had a speech all planned for Suzy and rehearsed it in the mirror. I wanted her to be as happy as Mum and Dad had been. When Friday came and she arrived at the house, she dropped her bags at the door and followed me through to the kitchen to make a cup of tea. Before I could even get the kettle on I heard her exclaim,

'What the . . . Kate, what's this? Are you pregnant? Oh my God, you're pregnant aren't you! Oh my God. Oh my God. No way. Seriously?'

Spinning around in disbelief, it took me a second to answer. Then I clocked it. She'd seen a juicing book I had open on a recipe called 'Bun In The Oven Juice', which was packed with essential prenatal vitamins.

'Oh Suze, I was just about to tell you.'

I couldn't believe I had blown my cover!

She said it again, 'You're pregnant!'

She stood stock still, in shock. I hugged her tight then grasped her shoulders and looked her in the eye.

'Yep, we're having a baby.'

She smiled cautiously.

'Are you sure?'

'Yes I'm sure. We've got a scan booked for tomorrow actually. I was wondering if you wanted to come with us?'

She started jumping up and down on the spot.

'Oh my God. Oh my God. Oh my God. YES. I'd love to. PLEASE let me be part of that. Are you kidding? Of course I want to go with you!'

I hugged her again.

That night she talked about nothing else.

'I'm going to be an aunty. Mum and Dad are going to be grandparents. Oh my God. Paul's going to be an uncle. Ha, an uncle. This is so weird. You're having a baby. An actual baby.'

Suzy had hyped James and me up to fever pitch excitement by the time we got to the hospital the following morning. The three of us looked at one another as the sonographer squeezed the cold wet gel on my tummy for the ultrasound. The second I heard the heartbeat, my soul leapt. We all fell silent, watching and listening as we saw a tiny bean appear on the screen. Suzy held one of my hands and James held the other, and we all had tears streaming down our faces.

We went away with the very first picture of our baby – our little peanut! I was ready to show it to Paul and Leah later that night over Skype, but instead, standing up, I lifted my top and showed them what could have passed as bloating but they guessed instantly it was the beginning of a baby bump. There were tears of joy on both sides of the Atlantic.

Chapter Twenty-Eight

After telling Paul, I next shared the baby news with Kay. After first crying with happiness she then started listing all the things Noah had outgrown which I could have for my baby. Ever practical, ever emotional, ever Kay! I was so excited that we'd be raising our children together and that we would have one another to rely on as we worked our way through our new roles as mums.

A couple of weeks after the scan, I was in the garden enjoying the evening summer sunshine while James put together some new outdoor furniture. Dinner was in the oven and we'd both been back from work for about an hour. It seemed a perfectly normal day.

I was on the phone to Mum, having our daily chat. I'd texted her a funny picture of my non-existent bump that morning and we were planning our next weekend together.

She had recently told me she'd been feeling unwell for a few weeks and was plagued by stomach problems that wouldn't go away, so her GP had arranged for some tests. I had been telling her I thought she probably had irritable bowel syndrome, or something like it, and we were waiting to see if I was proved right.

'I had my scan today,' she told me.

'Is it IBS? What do you have to cut out? Gluten?'

'No, Kate, it's not IBS.' She paused and I sensed straight away she had something big to tell me. 'They suspect it might be cancer.'

The world stopped, I didn't hear anything else she said after that. All I could think was that she was my best friend, my most trusted confidante in the entire world, the person who was with me always. She'd given me hope, coped with my despair, raised me, made me, saved me. I couldn't believe she could be ill. The thoughts were coming too thick and fast. I cut them all off, tears starting to roll down my cheeks.

'What?? Please no. Mum, please. I can't believe we're having this conversation.'

I could barely breathe.

'It's not fair, you don't deserve this. You can't be ill, you're Mum. *I'm* the one who is meant to be ill. *You're* the one that's supposed to be well. Please, Mum. Not you. I need you.'

I was choking on the words and she tried her best to calm me down.

'Kate, love, do you want to take a minute? I know it's a big thing to take on board. You can call me back if you like?'

I struggled to speak. 'Thanks, Mum. I'm finding it hard to talk right now. I'll call you back . . . I love you.'

Just five minutes earlier, everything had been seemingly fine; our family was perfect when I had woken up that morning. Hearing my sobs, James rushed over and gathered me in a hug, waiting for me to explain.

'They think my mum's got cancer . . .' We held tight to one another.

Despite the warm sunshine, I felt my skin rise into goosebumps. My mind raced: there had to be something I could do to make things better, some answer that would fix everything. After all, I'd been fixed when I was very, very broken, so I knew it was possible; there must be something practical that would help mend things and get everything back on track.

Reaching deep to find the Piper strength that Mum and Dad had instilled in me, I went into Practical Katie mode and ran upstairs to switch on the laptop. I started Googling everything I could on colon tumours and cancer. I'd once been on a juice retreat in Portugal where they talked a lot about their belief that juicing can help beat disease. I found lots of potentially cancer-beating recipes online using wheatgrass, spirulina, cabbage, broccoli, spinach – all the green vegetables. I Googled tonnes of superfoods, and ordered the best juicer I could find online to be delivered to their house.

Next stop: Ocado. I ordered them enough fruit and veg to start a market stall so Mum would be all set to make the juices herself. I ordered a book which promised to help you drink your way to health then sent her an email with a whole diet plan for juices that are reported to help shrink tumours and help the bowel, and instructions on what to avoid.

Two hours later I switched off the computer, exhausted and tense but sure I'd fixed everything. I'd been my usual practical self. Now everything could return to normal. Couldn't it?

That night I didn't sleep. I thought back to the hours Mum spent holding my hand while I drifted in and out of consciousness after the attack. The litter pickups she'd taken us on when we were kids to help clean up our local park during the summer holidays. The way she'd kissed my knees better when I fell out of the apple tree in the back garden while trying to climb as high as Paul.

The way she'd helped me make a Victoria sponge when I was eight for the competition at the local village fete. How she allowed me to butcher her wardrobe for the annual Piper nativity play I insisted on directing every year as a child. The way she lovingly compiled a scrapbook of photographs recording every single step of my recovery. The way her eyes had filled with tears of pain when I'd taken the stand during the trial after I was attacked, and how they'd filled with tears of joy when I won my Pride of Britain Award four years later.

I lay there in the dark holding my tummy and wondering how it was possible that I'd be bringing a life into this world while Mum would be fighting for hers at the same time. I was celebrating my good news while she was being crushed under the weight of her bad news.

I couldn't help but think about the practicalities too. I know what it's like to be in hospital with very little dignity. I know how it feels to lose your hair. I remember having a colostomy bag and being washed by strangers – even by male nurses because of staff shortages. I didn't want her to go through that. She always wears make-up and does her hair; she takes a huge amount of pride in her appearance. I didn't want my mum to be stripped of all the things that make her feel beautiful.

Mum had already spent too much time in hospital as a visitor for me; why did she now have to go back as a patient? I wanted to do all I could for her, as she had done for me, including take her place.

Though we didn't have an official diagnosis yet, the enormity of the news made me confront the fact that she wouldn't be with me forever. Despite being twenty-nine, until that night I'd taken for granted that she would always be at my side for every test and every triumph. But she wouldn't. Even if she beat this, at some point I'd have to face the inevitable. In fact, I'd never thought about any of my family not being there to stand shoulder-to-shoulder with me as I face the world; they have been the most remarkable and loving support system, and one I give thanks for every single day.

There will be many challenges ahead of me still, including the day my attackers come out of prison. I'd always imagined my family would be right there beside me, holding my hands when it happened, but that night I began to wonder whether they actually would be.

My parents are the only people on earth who really know what I've been through. They're the only ones who saw it all. The only ones who lived it with me, day in, day out. Not even Paul or Suzy know the extent of what my parents and I experienced together and what they had to cope with.

They saw things even I didn't see, spent hours looking at me and soothing me when I wasn't allowed a mirror. We've been through a shared tragedy and have such a strong bond. We're a raft of survivors all clinging to one another and keeping each other afloat in dark moments, and I've really come to rely on that. I only hoped I could give half as much back to Mum as she had given to me.

It felt like my heart was breaking.

I kept thinking about the saying, 'For every life that comes into the world, one leaves it.' I was pregnant. What if my baby's life beginning meant my mum's had to end? My mum had lost her own mother six months after she gave birth to Suzy. Now I was pregnant and Mum was ill. Would history repeat itself? It'd be too cruel a twist.

I didn't want to have a baby without her. Who would answer all my questions about how I should help it sleep through the night, and when I should wean it, and all the other questions a daughter has for her mum when she has her own baby? I spent the entire night veering between trying to be practical and feeling sad, overwhelmed and helpless.

I phoned Suzy the next morning. She didn't answer but texted me minutes later saying she wasn't ready to talk about it. I called Paul at his home in Colorado. He was trying to put a rational, practical head on, though I could tell by his voice that he was also secretly sick with worry but perhaps didn't want to say so to his little sister.

While we waited another fortnight for the rest of Mum's test results, we all felt like we were trapped in limbo. Despite talking every day, we never spoke about the impending results. Mum asked me endless questions about how I was feeling and how the baby was, suggesting long baths to help with the daily rib discomfort that I was starting to get.

I felt like she was avoiding any mention of her own situation on purpose, but then I wondered whether my pregnancy hormones had made me an emotional mess, misreading the situation as something much more sinister than it might really be.

None of us had anything to say to each other. No words were going to change the situation so we just steeled ourselves. The Piper strength and determination that had become the trademark of our family came to the fore once again. We all knew that if the worst happened, we'd deal with it. There was no point thinking about it now.

But just looking into Dad's tired eyes you could see how scared he was, for himself and for his wife. Dad tried to be really optimistic. Both of them wanted to protect us from the worst. In their eyes we were the kids and we needed to be sheltered from the bad news. But I just wanted to know so I could make plans with how to deal with it mentally.

I found out a couple of weeks later that the very day I told them I was expecting, they had planned to tell me Mum's news. On the way to meet us in the car, Mum and Dad had their inkling that I had some news of my own so they both promised they wouldn't utter a word before I'd spoken up. They told me they'd not wanted to ruin my happiness that day but in a way I wish they'd had the courage to tell me so I could have supported them earlier.

In the days that followed, Paul, Suzy and I continued along in our own worlds, waiting for the call. Then it came. The scan results confirmed what we'd all come to expect: it was cancer. There were no words. Nothing that could change the diagnosis. No taking it back or rubbing it out. We'd prepared for the worst but hoped for the best . . . but it wasn't to be.

The doctors booked Mum straight in for a partial bowel removal before starting her on an aggressive three-month course of chemotherapy to tackle the other tumours in her liver. They told us that if the tumours didn't shrink in response to the treatment, they might have to operate again in the New Year. But if everything went according to plan, after another three-month course of chemotherapy, she'd be free of cancer. It was going to be pretty gruelling for her. She tried her best to stay strong for all of us.

'The doctors know what they're doing and I'm in safe hands, Kate, don't worry.'

Even in the wake of such devastating news, she tried to coax a smile out of me, I'm sure to make me think things weren't as bad as they sounded.

'I just . . . I just want to make sure you're okay with everything?'

'Yes of course I am, love. Now, how's that bump doing?'

I knew my baby was motivating Mum to keep going and giving her something to fight for, but it seemed so horrendously unjust. But then I remembered once again that life doesn't always happen how you want or expect it to. You can't always be there to protect the ones you love. You can't always take away their pain and fear and hurt. You can't always make things better, no matter how much you may want to. Sometimes you just have to stand beside them, shoulder to shoulder, and let them know they're not alone in whatever they're facing.

The day of the first operation, we all held our breath until Dad called to tell us she was out of surgery and that the doctors were pleased with what they'd removed. I headed to the hospital as soon as he got off the phone. She was still groggy and tired when I got there but visiting her and seeing for myself that she was awake made things seem like they were going as well as they possibly could be.

I still wished I could take her place, and as she started to recover, I had to keep reminding her how to be a patient. She was understandably impatient to be discharged, bored in bed all day and frustrated at not being in charge for once. It was a relief for everyone that Mum then had a few weeks at home to concentrate on her recovery before the next part of the treatment, the chemotherapy, was due to begin. We all knew she had a long road ahead but it gave us much-needed time to draw breath, spend precious time with her and ready ourselves for the next round.

Chapter Twenty-Nine

I spent the following weeks seesawing between excitement and happiness at the baby growing safe and well in my tummy, and a fearful paranoia about Mum's future.

The doctors were positive about her treatment plan and she was recovering well at home with me, Paul and Suzy calling constantly to nag her to get enough rest and not try to do too much.

I'd hardly been thinking about much other than Mum and had just got off the phone to her one morning when Joanne called out of the blue and said she'd had an unbelievable request from M&S.

'Katie, this is amazing. They want you to be part of their new autumn/winter ad campaign for 2013.'

'Me? No. Seriously? I'm not a model, why would they want me? Are you sure you heard right? Marks and Spencer?'

'Yes, positive. There's more. The campaign is called Leading Ladies and they're asking all kinds of remarkable women to take part. It's not just a straightforward "sit there and smile", this is about empowerment, about being a leading lady in British society. They want to meet you to explain the campaign next week.'

I had to let it sink in. The biggest and oldest high-street fashion retailer in the UK wanted me. To help front their campaign. With all the extremes that were going on around me, this was just one more unbelievable bit of news.

My response was immediate. 'Wow, what an honour! That's incredible! Tell me more...' I called Mum and told her straight away.

Two days later I was on the way to the M&S head office. I called Mum en route; she was gearing herself up for her first dose of chemotherapy and as usual was refusing to let any of us dwell on her condition.

'Good luck, Kate,' she said. 'Promise you'll call me as soon as you're out of the meeting to let me know how it went?'

'Of course, Mum. Mum?'

'Yes?'

'How are you? I mean, how are you feeling?'

'I'm fine, love, just going out in the garden so if I don't answer the landline, try my mobile.'

Once I got to M&S the scale of the campaign became clear. They told me the names of the other women involved: dancer Darcey Bussell; actress Dame Helen Mirren; Olympic boxer Nicola Adams; artist Tracey Emin; model Karen Elson; CEO of Save the Children International, Jasmine Whitbread; Nurse of the Year Helen Allen; US *Vogue*'s creative director, Grace Coddington; author Monica Ali; singer Laura Mvula and . . . me. I was speechless as one of the creative guys explained the campaign further.

'We want this to speak to women of all ages and backgrounds. We want to let people know what clothes mean to you. What does being a woman in society mean to you? What are your beliefs, your morals; who are you?'

They really wanted it to be a thought-provoking campaign.

I called Mum the minute I got outside into the warm summer sunshine and rattled off the names of the other women. I could hear her repeating them out loud to Dad who was standing beside her.

'I mean, I never thought I'd even be in the same sentence as influential women like Helen Mirren and Darcey Bussell, let alone on the same shoot as them. Can you believe it, Mum?'

'We're both very very proud of you. When's the shoot?'

'In a few days and guess what else? Annie Leibovitz is shooting it. You know, the mega-famous celebrity photographer from *Vanity Fair*?'

I knew they were happy for me but I was desperate to ask her again how she was doing, to tell her I was there if she ever wanted to talk. But I also knew I didn't need to say it out loud. She knows just how much I love her and exactly what she means to me. Mum always knows what's in my head. Sometimes even before I do.

'Mum?'

'Yes, Kate?'

'I love you.'

'I love you too, darling.'

On the day of the M&S shoot, the call time to be on set was 7am. The location? A field in the middle of nowhere. Determined not to be late, I'd left home in plenty of time and turned up a little early. I was struggling with morning sickness but no one other than my family knew about my pregnancy yet and I was keen to keep it that way. The set was packed with runners, assistants, the 'creatives', agents, celebrities – you name it. It felt more like a film set than a photo shoot.

Two giant Winnebago vans were parked side by side and I was ushered into one and straight into a make-up chair. I was wracked with nerves and was sure nobody would know why I was there, and that everyone would think I was some weirdo who'd had far too much cosmetic surgery that had gone wrong. Taking a sip of the tea I'd been given, I looked over to the space beside me.

'Hi, I'm Darcey . . .'

I nearly fell out of my chair. 'Yes, oh, erm, hi! Hi, I'm Katie.'

I squeezed my eyes closed, trying to take a picture of the moment in my mind forever. I, Katie Piper, was sitting next to Darcey Bussell, one of the most revered ballet dancers in the world.

'Hi, you must be Katie? I'm Tracey.'

I opened my eyes and leaning over me was Tracey Emin. The previous evening, I'd told James I was terrified of meeting her. She always seemed so confident, so self-assured. I was positive she'd be in charge, smoking, shouting and swearing.

'Yes, hi.'

Helen Mirren had brought her husband with her. She was incredibly charming and staggeringly beautiful in equal measure and made us all feel relaxed.

Nicola Adams and I talked loads about diet and exercise. I told her about my half-marathon and she extolled the virtues of boot camp.

Nurse of the Year Helen Allen was a real inspiration for everyone there. Helen is a highly trained cardio-thoracic nurse, and as part of her training spent time in Zambia, where she was born. She has not only continued to work with Zambian nurses, but she started a charity that is devoted to raising awareness about HIV and poverty there. The charity also offers opportunities for people from the UK to volunteer in Zambia, and they work closely with schools and universities in the UK to form a strong network between people here and in Zambia, to help shape and influence one another's lives. We all knew she was the real superstar of the shoot.

As I was being made up, Annie Leibovitz popped in and introduced herself to me and told everyone in the trailer we'd be ready to start shooting in just over an hour. Hair and make-up done, and clothes laid out ready to go on at the last minute, I started hovering near her.

Annie is such a legend, so I wanted to see how she worked, how she commanded a set, how she made everything look so beautiful – and how she'd become one of the most celebrated photographers in the world. Dignity, creativity and grace beamed from her every movement, every comment.

Within minutes I could see that she gets the very best out of everybody, from runners to models, by making them feel comfortable with one another. She'd put us all into as small a place as she could, just two trailers, to give us no choice but to interact with one another, connect and start getting on. We had all started bonding within minutes of being there and she knew that energy would show in the final shots. Seeing her work was so inspiring: her attention to detail, her passion and patience all paid off in getting great shots for the campaign.

'Okay, everybody ready?'

Soon we were all in the middle of the field under bright blue skies. It was searing hot weather and we were all dressed in autumn and winter clothes. Annie directed us one by one – where to stand, how to sit – making sure we all relaxed.

'We're just trying things out; I'm not shooting yet. Katie, do you want to try sitting at the front on the floor, leaning to one side? Tracey, you sit next to her on the other side.'

We assumed our positions. Unfortunately I plonked myself down straight on top of a giant nettle patch. Typical!

'Okay guys, that all looks perfect, hold it.'

Everyone else was in position, so I couldn't move else I'd mess up the shot. Annie started shooting, and I forced a smile even though I was in agony. It was so painful! I was being stung through my tights and every time I tried to reposition myself to make it better, it just made it worse.

Despite needing dock leaf after dock leaf to ease the stings when we wrapped, I loved every single second of being among all these amazing women. That anyone thought I deserved to be there felt really empowering, which helped take my mind off the morning sickness I was also feeling and the zapping pain of being stung.

Now, to be shot by one famous photographer was more than anything I could have dreamed of, but to be shot by both Annie Leibovitz *and* David Bailey in the same fortnight – who between them are responsible for some of the most iconic images of the last century – was nothing short of mind-blowing.

I'd been asked to pose for a piece in *Fabulous* magazine, but had only been told a few days beforehand that it would be David Bailey taking the pictures. I was still on a high from the M&S shoot when I turned up at his studio the following week.

David has shot The Beatles and Kate Moss more times than you can count, as well as every notable supermodel since the 60s. He's also responsible for one of the most famous portraits of Princess Diana. But when I met him, he showed me some images he'd taken in rural East Africa; he'd spent weeks out there shooting soldiers ravaged by war. His skill for knowing what makes a striking photo, whether the subjects are traditionally beautiful or not, is breathtaking.

Before we met, I'd heard about his reputation for being blunt and straightforward. They used to be traits I admired, but when you're facially disfigured, bluntness does very little for your self-esteem. Knowing I was going to have my make-up done, I walked in to the studio fresh-faced, with everything on show. He strode over and looked at me closer, examining every line and crease on my face, acknowledging the damage my attackers had done, but complimenting me on the fact I'd come out the other side. He was so matter-of-fact about it that for some reason I didn't feel offended. He was there to document my appearance and so it seemed okay that he'd commented on how I looked.

'I really wanted to photograph you. You're still so beautiful. Your bone structure is amazing.'

I didn't know what to say. I thought about all the other women who had graced his lens before me and couldn't help but wonder whether what we accept as traditional beauty isn't starting to change.

I could feel knots beginning to form in my tummy. The nerves and morning sickness were getting the better of me, and as if he knew I needed to compose myself, David soon turned his attentions from me and onto the emerging racks of clothes, which were fast filling up with a nautical theme. I heard him erupt.

'If I see any more stripes I'm going to be sick. Twiggy did it once, it can't be done again. I wish people would just stop trying to copy it. The picture is all about Katie, not about her hair or her clothes.'

He was so assertive about what he wanted, I didn't know what to say or where to look.

The make-up artist agreed on a fairly neutral palate for my make-up. David shoots on a closed set and so the second she was done, he ushered everyone out.

'Right everyone, Katie and I are ready, out you go.'

He lit a cigarette and started hovering inches from my face, reapplying some powder from a compact he had in his pocket.

My eyes started itching like crazy – they're sensitive at the best of times, but having Marlboro Red smoke drifting into them was agony. And being pregnant (although to be fair to David he didn't know that), I wasn't thrilled about breathing in smoke, so I held my breath until he returned to his camera. He stood back, clicking the shutter several times before adjusting the settings slightly and going again.

'Right, that's one shot down, shall we take a break?'

He opened up the set again and I found myself flicking through *Vogue* with him.

We stopped on a picture of one of the most famous super-models in the world.

'Shot her the other week, can't remember her name but she was a pain. Don't know what the fuss is about, she's a shortarse too.'

He asked me about the M&S campaign and told me about hanging out with Grace Coddington when they were younger.

By the end of the shoot I adored him. Yes, he's brutally honest, but at least you know what you're getting and exactly where you stand with him. When I got home, I was exhausted and stank of fags but it was all worth it for a one-on-one studio session with David Bailey.

I loved the shots when the magazine came out a few weeks later. They were really honest and stripped back, not like anything I'd seen of myself before. He'd been right in being so assertive about what would work – it had, and his shots remain some of my most treasured.

I could hardly wait for the M&S campaign to launch but I had to keep it strictly secret for three months after it was shot. But I had more than enough to keep me busy while the pictures were being edited. I was days away from the judging date for the Pride of Britain Awards and was busy again with Channel 4. They'd commissioned me for a series called *Bodyshockers*, in which I'd interview people who'd altered their image dramatically through choice, but who now had regrets. From full-body tattoos to piercings and cosmetic surgery, there was plenty of groundwork to be done to find startling and unusual case studies. And with the filming planned to take place all over the UK, plus one trip to Magaluf, the schedule was hectic to say the least. It was going to be tricky to keep my morning sickness at bay and continue hiding the fact that I was pregnant. I was still a fortnight away from the twelve-week mark, but I wanted to get past it by a week or two before I went public and shared with the world that I was going to be a mum.

Chapter Thirty

By September 2013 I had spent weeks reading and re-reading every entry for the Pride of Britain Awards, making notes, lists and crib sheets to ensure I absorbed the details of each and every person's journey. I was looking forward to spending a day in London with the other panellists, choosing from the very worthy nominees.

However, I had been asked to attend a TV industry event up in Scotland that same morning to chair a debate about Channel 4's programme *The Undateables*. It all went fine but my eyes were glued to the clock, desperate to get to the airport on time so that I didn't miss the Pride of Britain judging and let anyone down. The minute the debate finished, I ran as fast as I could to get a taxi to the airport.

My flight back to Heathrow was at 11 o'clock and I had to be in a central London hotel to meet my fellow judges by 1 o'clock. I knew I was cutting it fine but as long as we took off on time, I was confident I'd make it. Luck was on my side and we landed in London bang on schedule. I sprinted again for a taxi, with a hidden pregnancy bump and wearing stiletto heels, and arrived at the hotel looking a little dishevelled, only to be greeted by a cluster of paparazzi who had assembled to snap pictures of the judges as we went in for our long day. But while I may have been unprepared for the paps, I was more than ready for the task at hand.

The judging panel was chaired by *Mirror* editor Peter Willis and included Aled Jones, David Weir, Michael Owen, Denise Lewis, Carol Vorderman, Chief Constable of West Midlands Police Chris Sims, President of the Royal College of Nursing Andrea Spyropoulos, ITV News' Mark Austin, ITV's Jeremy Phillips, Marco Ivone of Lidl and *Mirror* Editor-in-Chief Lloyd Wembley.

By the time the sun went down on a long afternoon of debate and discussion, we all knew we'd made the right choices – hard as that was, with so many extraordinary and deserving unsung heroes. The whole experience left me feeling uplifted and exhilarated, and reconfirmed how much I really do love the Pride of Britain Awards – they celebrate the strength of the human spirit and give us new role models: people who are completely determined to make the world a better place. I was so proud to have been a part of the selection committee, but keeping the results secret until the ceremony in October was going to be hard.

Keeping secrets seemed to be a bit of a theme of late. I had managed to get through weeks of intense work without having to let on about my pregnancy to anyone but my family, but finally, having had to keep that under wraps (literally!) along with the M&S campaign and who we'd given the Pride of Britain Awards to, I could reveal my own news.

At last it was time for another scan to confirm I had made it through the sometimes-risky first trimester. I was now itching to share the news about my baby with the world. At the time, I was writing my column for the *Daily Mirror* and the morning it was due to be revealed in the paper, I tweeted about it. The response was overwhelming and unexpected. I wasn't prepared for the huge outpouring of love and warm wishes that came my way over the next forty-eight hours. Thousands of lovely people tweeted to wish me luck and happiness, and to say they'd shed a tear of joy for me when they heard the news.

I never expected my news to evoke such emotions in others, not least from people who didn't know me personally. I made sure to take screen shots of as many tweets as I could, and printed them out for a scrapbook of pregnancy memories that I'd started making.

It was a really happy time, and though I was excited about having gone public about the baby and was touched by all the support I was getting, all I could think about was Mum. She had just started her three-month course of chemotherapy when the M&S campaign launched in autumn 2013, and having recovered from the bowel operation so brilliantly, her liver op had been tentatively scheduled for January 2014. So far she'd only had one session of chemo, so the side effects hadn't yet kicked in. She was so excited about the campaign and was proud to see me in the posters, which were all over the place, on billboards and in stores: Katie Piper, Burns Survivor and Charity Campaigner. She so sweetly texted me pictures whenever she spotted one. It was good to feel like I might be providing even the slightest distraction for her, but I always wanted her to let me do more.

Despite her medical treatment, we all wanted to keep things as normal as possible, for Mum's sake, such as getting together as a family for my thirtieth birthday. James had organised a huge party for me at a venue near our house, which he had been planning for months. Mum and Dad were coming up to stay over and join the celebrations, and it felt like a big deal for all of us. Also, turning thirty meant leaving behind the decade in which I was attacked, so this birthday more than others felt like a huge turning point, a milestone none of us would forget.

I planned to show Mum a beautiful book some of my close Twitter followers had made for me and sent to the Foundation as a birthday present. I'd spent years communicating with all of them; many had come along to my book signing and they were always the first ones to congratulate me on any good news they read about me. They each had their own story: some were burns survivors living with disfigurement, while others wore their scars inside their hearts.

They'd spent months taking turns to write notes in the book, saying what I meant to them and how I'd helped them, each signing with their Twitter handle before posting the book on to the next person in the chain. They'd included pictures they liked of me and tied the whole thing up with ribbon. This extraordinary book remains one of the most remarkable, thoughtful and generous things anyone has ever given to me. Their words and notes were so poignant, and the great effort they'd gone to in making it for me brought tears to my eyes.

Hearing Mum and Dad's car on the driveway, I placed the book on the sideboard until we'd settled down. As they bundled through the door with a bag brimming with presents, I could feel my excitement starting to build.

'Mum, how are you feeling? You look great.'

'I'm fine, Kate. Your dad's been fussing, don't you start too.'

I kissed her and took the bag of presents from Dad. He also handed me a pile of post that had been delivered to their house. I still use Mum and Dad's address for a lot of official correspondence so they bring me a bundle whenever they see me.

The first few letters were general circulars, but the last one was a brown envelope. I'd been telling James to take Mum and Dad's bags upstairs, and while he did I started opening the post as I made my way to the kitchen to put the kettle on. What I saw as I opened the brown envelope stopped me dead. Inside was a pristine piece of white paper, on which was my name, the logo for Her Majesty's Prison Service, and in foreboding black letters, the name of the man who'd thrown acid in my face. I couldn't read any further.

I started crying, gasping in deep breaths to try and calm myself down.

'Dad . . .'

'What is it, love?'

I looked up at him, handing over the letter. Mum started reading it with him.

'Alright, Kate. Okay, love, calm down. Let's see what it says.'

Mum put her hands on my shoulders. I felt like I was going to faint and she rubbed my back while Dad read to the end of the letter.

My head was exploding with worry and questions that flashed through my mind like lightning bolts. 'Have they escaped? Are they coming to get me? What's happening??' I hadn't felt terror like that for a long time, but I tried to hold it together and keep the panic mostly to myself. I didn't want to upset everyone – it was meant to be a weekend of celebrations, a happy time spent all together, and tonight was my big party. But being confronted with this reminder of my deepest fears was so frustrating and upsetting, and I couldn't help it when I started to cry.

'Kate, listen.' Dad spoke to me in his calmest voice. 'He's still in prison, they both are. But according to this, Stefan is eligible to apply for a change to the terms of his sentence.'

'What does that mean?' I pleaded. 'Dad? I don't understand.'

Dad scanned the letter again. James rushed downstairs and held my hand while Dad read on further.

'It means he can apply to go to a lower security prison or he can apply for eligibility for parole.'

'But what will that mean for me? For us?' I felt helpless, knowing there was probably nothing we could do to stop this.

'I don't know, love. It says to phone them if we want to have a meeting.'

Mum and Dad exchanged a look, and they both held me while I tried to pull myself together. As I tried to calm myself down, I told myself that my attackers already owned enough of me, and I promised myself I wouldn't let them take my thirtieth birthday weekend away from me too.

I breathed deeply until the panic subsided, putting the letter in my diary, and refused to read it myself until my birthday weekend was over. I took that moment to show Mum the book from my Twitter friends, and it helped give me strength too.

As it happened, this was my first birthday since the attack five years before that I'd been able to celebrate properly on the actual day. For the first one, in 2009, I had been giving evidence in court and wasn't in a good frame of mind for celebrating, and on every birthday since I'd had hospital appointments for release operations, grafts or to have scar tissue removed from my throat and nostrils to help me breathe. I could have rescheduled any one of them, but instead had simply decided to celebrate my birthday before or after the actual date.

I spent hours getting ready, wanting to look perfect for my big night. Fortunately the vintage-style flapper dress and gold strappy heels I'd chosen months before still fitted over my growing bump. Mum, Dad, James and I shared a cab to the venue, and I was both nervous and excited all the way there as James squeezed my hand. There were over a hundred guests who had been invited: friends, cousins, aunts, uncles, colleagues from Channel 4 and the foundation, even wonderful Paul, who flew all the way over from Colorado, but James had kept me in the dark about pretty much everything else, and there were some wonderful surprises in store for me.

James's care and attention to detail was astonishing. He had spent hours putting together a playlist of all my favourite songs and had secretly booked the musicians from our favourite restaurant to play before a DJ took over. He had even sourced mini burgers and mini hotdogs (two things I'd been craving during pregnancy) and had the whole venue decorated with tea lights.

He had even put up a huge corkboard inside the room, and had asked everyone to bring pictures of themselves with me, which they pinned up. What I saw as it filled up took my breath away. Family members had pictures of me as a child, schoolfriends had dug out pictures of me as a teenager, while colleagues I'd befriended since the attack brought pictures of me at events. Seeing my friends, and my life, in pictures like this was so much fun. I stood for ages poring over every picture and enjoying every memory.

Since I talk (a lot) for a living, I figured everyone had already heard enough from me, so I'd asked Paul to do a speech. Towards the end of the meal he stood up to speak, and the room fell quiet. I could feel myself getting teary before he even started. First he thanked Mum and Dad for all they'd done for us kids. His speech was split into three parts, one for each of my decades. He began.

'Now, I'm sure this won't surprise you, but many of the traits you see in Kate today are naturally the way she has always been. I thought back to our childhood and the following themes sum up what Kate was like growing up: the first is that the things children are normally cautious about didn't faze Kate at all. For example, while other children would peer over the edge of a swimming pool, anxious about getting in, Kate would just hurl herself into the deep end and worry about learning to swim later.'

Everyone laughed knowingly.

'The second is that when other kids fell down and hurt themselves they'd start crying, but Kate would pick herself up and just keep running with as much tenacity as she'd had before. And finally, while other children were happy to blend in and stay quiet, Kate would always be the one singing, dancing, talking and making people laugh. I think that each of you can still recognise those traits in the Kate you know today. They have made her the person she is and have got her to where she is now.'

I was incredibly moved. But being my big brother, of course he also took the opportunity to embarrass me by revealing I'd stolen clothes from his wardrobe so compulsively that Dad had put a padlock on it to protect Paul's prized Champion jumper. He also told everyone I'd thrown pillows and cushions out of the bathroom window to break my fall whenever I snuck – or rather, jumped – out of the house as a teenager.

The laughter subsided as Paul moved on to how much my life had altered in my twenties.

'We all know that things changed dramatically for Kate, and in the past five years she has held on to the qualities she showed as a child. She throws herself in at the deep end of new experiences, she picks herself up after a fall (and seriously, what a pick-up), and she has reached out to literally millions of people with her unique personality and desire to spread happiness (and to talk). I'm also extremely proud of her for achieving the constants and commitments in her life; she is now a homeowner, runs a charity, is in a committed relationship with a fantastic guy, and next year she will become a mother. I look forward to what the next ten years will bring. One thing's for sure: with Kate's personality of "throw yourself in, pick yourself up and spread the laughter", I'm looking forward to being a part of it.'

As the room broke into applause and everyone raised their glasses, I wiped tears from my eyes, hugging my family and James as tight as I could before blowing out the candles on my cake to yet more cheers. I was so incredibly touched to see so many of the people who make up my life in one room. Everyone who came to the party that night reminded me of the huge network of love, care and compassion that's got me through to where I am now, and which continues to help me every single day. The whole night was amazing, one of the best of my life.

But the party didn't end there. Everyone stayed and danced and drank until the early hours of the morning (except me, of course, who was on soft drinks all evening!). By 2.45am James was still going strong and throwing shapes on the dance floor, but I had worn a special pair of Louboutins to the party and by that time I was in agony, and I asked James to take me home. Waiting for the taxi I could barely keep my eyes open, but the thought of having a piece of the huge birthday cake I was carrying when we got home kept me going for the final stretch. I fell asleep in the wee hours of the morning in James's arms with a smile on my face and a deep sense of happiness in my heart.

Chapter Thirty-One

The next day, James and I had a quiet birthday lunch at home with Mum, Dad, Paul and Suzy. After they all went on their ways, my thoughts naturally drifted back to the letter from the Prison Service. Despite the years that had passed, the trials still felt so recent. I can still remember the smell of the courtroom, the wallpaper in the witness waiting area, all the sounds . . . It was hard to believe that the man who threw acid in my face had already served almost six years of his life sentence, or that he was eligible to apply for a change in the terms of his imprisonment. It had taken me nearly that long to feel like I had rebuilt my life after he and Danny had taken so much from me, and now this man's punishment might soon be over.

While tidying up the house, I thought 'I'm the one with the life sentence. Not him. He can change his identity, change his name, get a new job, a partner, move on, act like he never did it, but I can't. I can't pretend it didn't happen because it's all over my face. I can't change my appearance back, and I can't forget it.'

It surprised me to realise suddenly that during all the counselling I'd had for my recovery, not once did I ever talk to anyone about what I might go through if and when my attackers were released. I wanted to be angry at this omission, even though I knew that, just after the attack, we'd had no choice but to focus on the immediate emotional trauma I had sustained. First we'd had to get me functioning again on a very basic level, and that was a one-day-at-a-time task. The counselling I'd had after that had concentrated on bringing back together the emotional and rational parts of my psyche, which had been severed during the rape and the attack. My PTSD was so acute at the time that I even lost control of my bowels when a police officer simply showed me a picture of Stefan for identity purposes. After the attack, the sight of a man in a hoody, even just on TV, reduced me to a trembling wreck. A banging door would make me cower, covering my face, expecting Danny and Stefan to come and finish me off, despite the fact that I knew full well they were in custody and I was safe at home. There was no logical response in my brain and that had to be fixed first. So the truth was that, back then, it really wasn't the time to think about my attackers being released on parole. I wouldn't have been able to cope at the thought.

After getting over the initial impact of the letter, I spent the next ten days trying to find a good moment to call the Victim Contact Unit to discuss my concerns about Stefan's request. The letter constantly peeped out of my diary like a bleak reminder, but I didn't want to call them on the way to work and start the day by getting upset, and the last thing I wanted to contend with after a long day's filming or meetings at the Foundation was the emotional upheaval of having 'that' conversation. I also didn't want a call to ruin my evening, to follow me into the sanctity of my home, my safe place with James.

Eventually I just had to dig deep and pluck up the courage, calling them from my office in my house one morning just after James left for work. The conversation only lasted a minute or two – the person on the other end of the phone could only go as far as helping me to make an appointment at the unit in a week's time.

I asked Dad to come with me to the meeting. James offered but I felt he didn't need to hear some of the details they might go into, or maybe I wasn't ready for him to hear them just yet. Besides, Dad had been with me since day one.

Mum wanted to come too but she had a chemotherapy appointment which she couldn't miss. I'd been trying to stay calm in front of her since I'd received the letter. I knew she was as worried as I was, but I figured that keeping her in the dark about how I was feeling would help her focus on herself for once. Dad and I promised we'd come straight to the hospital after the meeting and tell her what had happened.

The Victim Contact Unit is a government-run office connected to the police which helps communicate with crime victims about their perpetrators, including when they are eligible for parole. Because they deal with those who committed, as well as those who are victims of crime, all the doors have intercoms and keycode locks. Once we got through the secured doors we were ushered into a bland meeting room with a long table and uncomfortable chairs. An official-looking woman with brown curly hair and a clipboard came in and introduced herself as a victim contact officer, and the meeting began.

'As you know from the letter we sent you, one of the men convicted of the crimes against you has become eligible to apply for a change to the conditions of his sentence. At this point, this is only a pre-application. If he's successful here, he can apply offi-cially in about six months' time. His options are to ask for a transfer to a lower-security prison, or for the right to apply for parole. If you choose to, you can write a personal statement that will stay in his file and that will be read by a parole board every time he makes an application. You can be as honest as you want to be in the statement. You can discuss how his release may affect you, your family and your future. You can detail how you've tried to piece your life back together since the attack, and your fears for your safety if he's released.'

I wanted to be sure I understood what she was saying.

'So, this is like the impact statement I had to write for the trial?'

She nodded yes, but then continued.

'But I should tell you now, if you do decide to write something, he has a right to read it. You can apply for non-disclosure, which means only the parole board and his barrister are allowed to read it, but in all honesty it's unlikely you will get it.'

I looked at Dad; his face was as incredulous and questioning as mine was. She went on to explain.

'It's your choice but I've worked here for nearly ten years and the only times I've seen it granted was for victims of terrorism. There's a strict set of criteria that have to be met in order for it to be withheld and I've only ever seen it in cases of national security.'

I could feel hysteria starting to rise within me but seeing I was getting upset the support officer's voice gently interrupted my thoughts.

'You don't have to write an impact statement if you don't want to. Your original personal statement from the trial is still on file. So if it's too traumatic, there are other options. If he's granted parole you could get a restraining order against him coming within thirty miles of your address.'

'But won't he need to know the area I live in for that?'

She nodded again. She was trying to be as sympathetic as she could be but her hands were tied by the system she had to enforce.

'He would know your street but not your house number. We could put a radius around where you work too.'

'I work all over London, all around the country sometimes.'

It all felt so hopeless. I looked at Dad then back at her. She took a deep breath.

'The other man appears to be more of a threat to you anyway, he's the one that would be more likely to come after you.'

I froze.

'Pardon?'

'I just mean of the two men jailed for your attack, this man is probably the less likely to attempt revenge.'

I'd managed to hold it together until she said that, but my ears began to burn and I felt my skin start to prick. I knew I was going to cry but there was so much rage inside me too. I could hear myself shouting through sobs.

'There'll be a murder inquest because when they get out they're going to kill me!'

Dad reached for my hand and I could see tears falling from his cheeks. I knew I'd upset him but I couldn't stop crying or shouting.

'There's nothing I can do! Nothing anyone can do. No one's going to listen to me and put them away forever until I become a tabloid news story: "*Acid Girl Killed By Attackers.*" When they kill me, you'll all admit they never should have been released and that they posed a serious threat. But by the time there's an inquest it'll be too late.'

I turned to Dad.

'I wish I'd been burned in a house fire or a car accident. At least a fire wouldn't come after me again, at least a fire wouldn't have a score to settle.'

He tried his best to calm me. 'Kate . . . Please . . .'

As I tried to compose myself, the victim contact officer spoke gently.

'You don't have to decide what to do now. Think about it. We're here if you want to have another chat at any point.'

After the meeting, Dad gathered me in a hug while we both cried tears of frustration, anger and fear. It felt like we'd gone a long way back down a path we didn't want to revisit. We didn't want Mum to know how upset we'd been, so we put a brave face on things. I reapplied my make-up in the car on the way back to the hospital, smiling when I saw her in the outpatients' ward, where she was hooked up to a chemotherapy machine.

'How did it go, Kate?'

I did my best to look her in the eye.

'You know, I'd rather not have been there, but it was okay.'

'Really?'

She turned to Dad like she knew I was lying.

'Yep. It was okay. Kate did great.'

I followed Dad's lead and told her there were options I could explore to reduce the possibility of him ever getting parole.

'It's just a case of taking it step by step, Mum.'

I leaned over and kissed her, saying, 'I'd better go, James is expecting me home.'

Dad walked me to the door and we hugged one another tightly before I turned and left.

Using my hands-free on the drive home, I made urgent appointments with my lawyer and the bank. That week I wrote a will, set up a trust fund for James and our unborn child, arranged life insurance and put a sum aside in a high-yielding account which would go some way to covering our child's education. Whatever happened, I wanted the people I loved to be taken care of forever.

Chapter Thirty-Two

I tried my best to put the meeting out of my mind while I was filming my next show for Channel 4, *Bodyshockers*, but it wasn't working terribly well. On one particular day I was doing short interviews with people in Camden Market about tattoos, body art and cosmetic surgery, and I'd just finished talking to two teenage girls when a man in a hoody walked towards me.

'Hi, you're Katie Piper aren't you? Can I get a picture?'

I jumped and stumbled backwards, then stood mute, rooted to the spot in a trance. My director gently shook my arm.

'Katie, are you okay?'

I closed my eyes and shook my head, trying to snap myself out of it.

'I'm sorry. Sorry.' I looked at the man in the hoody. 'Yes, I'm Katie, pleased to meet you.'

'Er, I didn't mean to interrupt, I watched your documentary and just wanted to say I think you're great and see if I could have a picture.'

The director let go of my arm, giving me a long sideways look to check I was alright with this. I nodded that I was fine. I spoke to the man for a few minutes, posed for photos and promised to reply to his tweet on Twitter. As we said goodbye and he disappeared into the crowd, my director came back over and took me to one side.

'Katie, is everything okay?'

'Yes, yes. All fine. I just . . . I was concentrating and he took me by surprise.'

She still didn't look convinced.

'Okay,' she said, 'I think we've got everything we need for today anyway. Why don't you get yourself home?'

Nobody but my family and James knew about the possibility of the acid thrower's release. I could feel it was affecting the bridge between the rational and emotional parts of my brain. As I made my way home, I berated myself for what had happened during filming.

'He only wanted a picture, Katie, and you reacted like he was holding a cup of acid. Your attacker hasn't even come out of prison and you've gone back to being the jumpy victim rather than the strong survivor.'

On my way home through London, I looked at the Christmas lights that had started to go up and watched the hundreds of faces I passed, seemingly oblivious to all the evil that goes on in the world around them. I forced myself to think about the worst-case scenario if he did get parole; being attacked the same way again. Looking at my reflection in the cab window, damaging, negative thoughts began to swirl around in my head.

'I could never cope again, I know I couldn't. I couldn't dig deep enough to recover again. If he's going to come out and do anything to me, I'd rather he killed me the day he's released. I don't want him to wait a couple of years before he does it. And I don't want to be attacked again and live through it. I don't want any more prolonged suffering. I have had enough of feeling like an empty shell. If something's going to happen I want it to happen straight away because living in fear is no life.'

Still staring at my scarred reflection as dusk fell outside, I felt completely and utterly alone.

'No one can help me. No one.'

When I got home, I ran myself a bath before getting into bed. James opened the bedroom door a few minutes later.

'You still awake?'

'Yeah . . .'

He came and sat on the edge of our bed. I told him about my panic attack in Camden.

'How can I walk down the street with our child when I know he's been released and could be anywhere? And I can't just freak over how someone's dressed or how they approach me, it'll be too scary for a small child . . . what am I supposed to do?'

James stroked my hair.

'We'll work through it. Don't worry. We'll all keep one another safe. That's what families do. We just need to be vigilant and not take any risks.'

I sat up, keeping my hand on my bump.

'James, I had acid thrown in my face at 5 o'clock on a busy London street in broad daylight. There were loads of other people around, how could I have been *more* safe? I wasn't walking along a dark alley at midnight. So how do I stop it happening again? It may be called the justice system, but there isn't a lot of justice in it for me. I look at my life with you and our future together as a family. Almost every day I feel like the door on the past has closed. But then something happens and I'm reminded of it all. *I can move on from it. I* can heal the physical scars and learn to live with the emotional ones. *I* can make my life as safe as I can. But I can't change that there are two men in the world who tried to ruin me, and they'll be free men one day.'

It was a sad and simple truth, and there wasn't much more we could say. James got ready for bed and crawled in beside me, and held me until I fell asleep.

Chapter Thirty-Three

I woke up feeling a little stronger for a good night's sleep, though everything was still playing on my mind. The Pride of Britain Awards ceremony was coming up the following week so I decided to make that my focus for the time being. I'd been so nervous the year before knowing I was receiving an award, but this year as a judge I could just relax and enjoy the night, which was a particularly welcome thought after the week I'd had.

There were many heart-warming, remarkable stories on the night, but the one that will stay with me forever was that of a little boy who is the epitome of triumph over adversity, to whom we gave the Child of Courage award. Eight-year-old Harley Lane nearly died of meningitis at the age of three. Not only did his heart stop three times, the septicemia he contracted in hospital resulted in the amputation of all four of his limbs. Despite these setbacks and his very young age, this smiley, determined little boy has shown no signs of stopping, and his many remarkable achievements include raising over £1,000 for the hospital that treated him by completing the 1.5-kilometre Bupa Mini Great Manchester Run. He even wants to be the first person with no legs to walk on the moon, and if there's anyone who could possibly make that happen, it'll be Harley.

Suzy and I spent ages talking to Harley's mum Samantha and dad Adam. Harley's confidence and cheeky personality are clearly a result of their strength and love.

They'd normalised his life, never calling undue attention to his differences or telling him he 'couldn't' do things, and as a result he'd never seen himself as different or disabled. It reminded me of my own parents, and made me aspire to be like them; to show unwavering support, unconditional love and undoubtable strength, no matter what life threw at them. I wanted my child to grow up strong, happy and invincible – just like Harley is.

The following morning, with thoughts of Harley still fresh in my mind, James and I went for our twenty-week scan. We had decided to find out the baby's gender and were excited and nervous. Previous scans hadn't been able to determine the sex, but we were both pretty sure we were having a son. Mum had my brother Paul first, and James had a big brother, so I was sure we'd follow suit.

'So you're sure you want to know, yes? You don't want it to be a surprise?' I checked with him.

'Kate, I'm positive it's a boy but yes, we'll get it confirmed.'

I laughed. 'I know, I'm sure he's a "he" too. They're also going to check all the organs and bones and measure everything to make sure he's developing ok. They said my bladder has to be full so they can see him better; can you pass me that bottle of water?'

Twenty minutes later we left the hospital reeling. Beaming but reeling. I spoke first.

'Uh, we're having a girl, James. How did that happen?'

'Yep. Not a boy. A girl.'

I don't know why we had been so convinced it was a boy, but we were. Everyone around us had been too. People had told me my bump was neat and all out front; all my colleagues were convinced I was having a boy. We hadn't even considered girls' names.

Regardless, we were so happy 'she' was growing perfectly, the technician told us that each little vertebrae in her spine was forming as it should, the blood was pumping in and out of her heart the right way, her little feet, tiny hands, and button nose were all visible. Clutching the printed scan to my heart, I closed my eyes and tried to imagine what she might look like when I finally got to meet her in a few months' time.

A million thoughts raced through my head about having a daughter as we weaved our way out of the car park. What if she's a tearaway like I was? What if she tries to pierce her own ear like I did? What will James say when she comes downstairs in a short skirt? And then my mind turned to more worrying things; what if she gets involved with an abusive boyfriend, like I did? I wondered whether we could ever keep her as safe as she was right then in my tummy; warm, protected and safe. The responsibilities of parenthood seemed immense as we drove our way home. We had a lot to think about.

Three days later my little girl-to-be and I were on the way to Oxford University, where I'd been invited to speak at the student union. It's a pretty prestigious invitation; previous speakers have been former prime ministers, world statesmen and women, bonafide game changers and trailblazers such as astronaut Buzz Aldrin, President Hamid Karzai of Afghanistan, American *Vogue* editor Anna Wintour, and even conspiracy theorist David Icke. I tried to calm my nerves as I made notes in the back of the car.

Standing in the Gladstone Room at Oxford University while I waited to be called into the library, I felt a huge weight of responsibility. I was about to address such bright, young twenty-somethings who were filled with hope and the feeling that anything is possible, and who would be some of tomorrow's leaders, thinkers and innovators.

Taking my place behind the podium, I cursed my choice of footwear. I'd not given enough thought to standing for an hour in six-inch Louboutins while five months pregnant, but once I got underway, my aching feet didn't seem to matter.

The intelligent questions they asked me after I spoke made this one of the most poignant talks I've ever done. I was astounded that with such a vibrant education on offer at one of the most important seats of learning in the world, they thought Katie Piper from Hampshire was worth taking the time to listen to.

As I gathered my coat to leave, a student motioned me over. He'd been at the back of the room making notes. He told me he'd been abused regularly by a family member while he was growing up. He told me he'd been thinking about counselling for some time, but after hearing my talk he finally decided he didn't want to be a victim anymore. 'I want to be a survivor, like you . . .' It was a powerful moment. We spoke for a few minutes. I thanked him for his honesty, squeezing his arm and wishing him all the luck in the world as I left.

On the drive back to London, with the streetlights whizzing by in a blur, I thought back to all the men and women I'd met and spoken to who had opened up to me over the years about their experiences. Every single day I hear people's incredible stories; people who decide to be survivors and start living for the moment, and for the future, rather than staying trapped in the past. Whether I'm stopped in the street or contacted by email or a tweet, hearing people say I helped them has restored the faith in humanity that my attackers tried to take away from me.

In the aftermath of my attack, I thought no one would ever relate to me ever again. I felt like a freak who would never be able to function in society. But instead I became part of a huge community of people who help one another, who want to get better, who strive to recover and who support one another on the path to recovery, wellness and happiness.

The stories I've heard over the years haven't always been easy to listen to. Some have left me feeling devastated and heartbroken, questioning why such evil exists in the world. But despite that, I'm always encouraged by people's tenacity and resilience, even when they're on their knees emotionally. They somehow find the courage, strength and determination to stand up and carry on.

Taking strength from the people who spoke to me after the lecture, I vowed not to let my attacker's potential parole ruin the final few months of my beautiful pregnancy. Until that letter arrived I'd been enjoying one of the most amazing periods of my life so far. Allowing something I ultimately couldn't control to drive me into fear, worry and confusion was out of the question.

I know I can't predict what will happen in the future. I can't know how things will pan out. None of us can. But I know that making today the best it can be is the best way to stay a survivor and not to become a victim again, so rather than focus on the past, on what has happened to me, I have to set my thoughts firmly on the future, and the good things that await me and my family.

Chapter Thirty-four

Vowing to have a festive period filled with positivity and love, I threw myself into making Christmas 2013 one to remember. The year so far had been a heady mix of rewarding and terrifying. On the one hand, I'd fallen in love and moved in with James, watched Kay become a mum and got pregnant myself. But on the other, Mum had been diagnosed with cancer and was still having chemotherapy, and was potentially facing a second operation on her liver at the start of 2014. Then there was the possibility that one of the men who attacked me would be granted parole some time in the next twelve months.

James and I had decided we'd invite our families for a big Christmas lunch, and since neither of us was exactly Jamie Oliver we thought we'd better get some cooking lessons, lest everyone go hungry on the day. I found a professional chef to give us private classes at home, and we really enjoyed our time learning something together with a big goal in mind.

We spent the week running up to Christmas making cupcakes, planning our timings and taking delivery of various food and presents for everyone. We'd planned everything with military precision and come Christmas morning I didn't think we could be more prepared. The lounge filled up fast and the glasses emptied just as quickly, and even though it meant everyone was quite tipsy when lunch was served an hour and a half late (blame the potatoes!), it was a wonderful time together as an extended family. After lunch, Dad and James took it in turns to massacre Elvis songs on the karaoke, before teaming up for what can only be described as the worst duet ever.

James and I had promised not to get one another anything – hosting Christmas dinner had cost enough, but neither of us kept our word. He bought me a beautiful handbag and I got him a DVD box set and some CDs from 'the bump'. And despite not yet being there in person, our baby girl received the most presents of all, including clothes, toys, pictures and wall hangings. She was already part of a family filled with love, devotion and excitement, and all looking forward to her arrival.

After a quiet New Year, we turned our focus to Mum. She was booked in for another scan in a fortnight to check the tumours on her liver after her first three months of chemo. We knew there were three possible outcomes: they'd shrunk so she wouldn't need a second operation, stayed the same, or they had grown and possibly spread further – in which case she'd need the operation to remove part of her liver and the scan would determine just how much.

On the day of the appointment, we waited anxiously as Dad took her in and promised to call the minute they got back from the hospital. After what felt like a lifetime, the phone rang.

'They haven't spread or got any bigger.'

I felt a hopeful surge.

'Dad, that's fantastic news, can I speak to Mum?'

'Hang on a minute, Kate.'

I could tell by his tone he didn't think the news was as good as I did.

'Why? What is it?'

'They haven't shrunk as much as they wanted them to. They're planning to remove half her liver next month. It's the aggressive surgery we were trying to avoid.'

I could tell they were disappointed with the results but, trying to be optimistic as they had been for me so often, I reminded him things could have been much worse. He passed the phone on to Mum. Typically, she wasn't worried at all about herself.

'Kate, whatever happens, it's bad timing for you and the baby. If I have the operation next month it'll take a couple of months to recover. They told me that as soon as I'm well enough, I have to start three more months of chemo, which means I have to stay close to home. It means I'll either be ill or recovering when you give birth.'

I wanted to put my arms around her.

'Mum, don't think like that. We can Skype every day and I can come down and stay as soon as I have her.'

'I know, love. I just wanted to be of more use, to take care of her so you could get some proper rest. It was a long time ago, but I remember how exhausting the early days are.'

My eyes filled with tears and by the time we got off the phone I couldn't hold them back. Mum. My mum. Still more worried about me than she was about her upcoming operation. Thinking back, I couldn't remember a single time where she'd put herself first. Ever.

I called Paul in Colorado the minute I knew he'd be awake. Within seconds he told me he was as worried as I was.

'I'm thinking of coming home so I can see her before the operation, or maybe I should stay for it? She's having half her liver removed, it's a big deal.' We both paused, then he said out loud what we were both sick with worry about. 'She might not even make it through.'

'Paul, do you really think she's that ill?'

I could feel my voice breaking. It was like we were little again and I was tugging on his T-shirt asking him to tell me everything would be alright after I'd watched a scary movie.

'I don't know, Kate. It's a huge procedure.'

I thought about moving back home temporarily and commuting to London for work, but I was nearly eight months pregnant and needed to be near my hospital in case I went into labour.

I was sick with worry when I went for lunch with my friends Sophie and Marty a few days later. I knew them both from my early days in TV and we used to live together, but Sophie had been working overseas for the last year and I hadn't seen Marty since my thirtieth birthday party. We were talking about Mum, the baby and bad timings when they both asked in unison when I was going to have a baby shower.

'I'm not having one, guys.'

Sophie piped up first, 'What? You have to have one.'

'You absolutely definitely have to have one,' chipped in Marty.

'No, I don't want one.' I told them. 'You're supposed to have baby showers a few weeks before the baby is due. If I leave it that late Mum won't be able to come because she'll be having her second operation.'

I had thought about organising one myself but had decided against it, partly due to being too busy and partly because I knew there was every chance Mum wouldn't be able to be there.

Sophie spoke first.

'So organise it now. Have it soon and your mum can come. She'll love it.'

'No, really Soph, even if I wanted to, I don't have the time to organise it at such short notice.'

'That's fine, we have the time. Marty and I will sort the whole thing. Give us a date you're free and a list of people you want to invite and we'll do the rest.'

Sophie had just relocated and was busy trying to find a place to live and a new job but being such an awesome friend, she still wanted to do this for me. After another twenty minutes of their nagging I finally relented. I smiled as I got a cab back to the office, thinking about how lucky I am to have people in my life that care about me so much.

One whirlwind week later, I was surrounded by all my best friends, and of course Mum. They'd all been mobilised at a moment's notice by Sophie and Marty, who had sorted the shower unbelievably fast. They had organised an afternoon tea in a local hotel and decorated the room brilliantly with pink balloons and banners saying 'It's a girl!', and made place cards for everyone for the table. They'd been right: Mum was the brightest I'd seen her in weeks – I could tell because she was being her usual, incredibly organised self. Sophie and Marty had put her next to me at the head of the table and she'd come armed with a digital camera and a notebook.

She whispered to me, 'Kate, as you open your presents, tell me who they're from and I'll write it down so you can do thank-you letters later.'

'Thanks, Mum.'

I squeezed her hand. Rubbing my bump, I told Mum just how lucky my daughter was.

'Look, she's not even here yet and there's a room full of people who are waiting to love her and meet her . . .'

Marty and Sophie had bought a blank book and decorated every page with hearts, bows and little elephants. Everyone passed the book around, writing the date they guessed the baby would be born, and what weight and length they thought she'd be, followed by a personal note for me and James. We had tons of chocolates that spelled out 'Congratulations', and toasted the baby with pink champagne. I had one small sip.

James came and picked me up from the hotel to help me bring home all the presents (and get lots of attention from my wonderful girlfriends), and despite getting stuck in horrendous traffic on the way home, nothing could wipe the huge smile off my face. With a back seat filled with presents, and a warm glow from the love of my friends, I grew even more excited about my daughter's impending arrival.

With my due date getting closer and closer, James and I finally started ordering the kit we hadn't got around to buying yet: a buggy, cot, bouncer, muslins, clothes – the lot. I ticked and cross-checked helpful lists given to me by friends who were mums to make sure we had everything we'd possibly need for her arrival and beyond. But all the while I shopped and prepared for this new life, I was so conscious of the fact that Mum was waiting for her liver operation. The doctors had to delay it because she'd caught the flu, so by the time she went in to hospital, it was the middle of February, and we all felt as if we had been waiting forever – both for Mum's op and for my daughter. It was all such unbelievable timing.

I called Mum on the morning of the op and told her I'd be at the hospital that evening to check on her. Watching the time on the clock slowly ticking by as she was in theatre, I couldn't imagine the emotions she must have felt as she waited for seven hours outside the operating theatre after my attack, not knowing whether I would live or die, but knowing I'd never look the same again. Now that I was about to be a mother of my own little girl, I felt an even greater sense of understanding about what torture it must have been for her, how helpless and desperate she must have felt, not being able to fix her child.

Finally, the call came from Dad. He sounded exhausted but I could tell instantly the operation had been a success. He told me that it had gone very well and that the surgeons were satisfied with the result, and that she'd fared very well under the anaesthetic.

I jumped in the car and tore over to the hospital. By the time I got there Mum was awake, although tired and groggy. I gave her a gentle hug. When the nurses brought round her medication, I slipped a few chocolate mini eggs into the tiny cup on top of her painkillers, and she gave me a sleepy smile.

In the follow-up appointments after her discharge from hospital, the doctors confirmed that the operation and her recovery had both been successful. They'd got all the tumours in her liver and it was time to start her on more chemotherapy. They scheduled a full-body scan for her to have later in the year to ensure that the cancer remained at bay and didn't spread, but for now she seemed well on the road to recovery.

Knowing Mum had come through the worst, I could now concentrate fully on having my baby. The doctors and I had to think carefully about how I would give birth because of several health issues. First, the scar tissue in my nose had thickened during the last eight months and my nostrils had contracted making them smaller, so was it impossible to take deep breaths. I was used to this happening and I usually just had an operation to take care of it, but a general anaesthetic was out of the question during pregnancy. So, with my compromised breathing, a natural birth was too chancy. Added to this, I have a scar on my stomach from where my feeding tube had been inserted after I was attacked, which had stretched during pregnancy and there was concern it could rupture if I ended up going past my due date.

With so many risks, the doctors scheduled a C-section for 14 March – one week and six days before my baby's due date. It meant that we would avoid the 27 March, the six-year anniversary of when I was raped. After months of coming to terms with that being her likely birthday, it was a relief that she'd actually end up being born on a different day.

I was calling Mum daily to see how she was, and as per usual she would turn the tables and talk about me and the baby, reminding me about things like packing plenty of nappies for the hospital and making sure James had enough change for the car park. So I thought a visit in person might get her to open up a bit about how she was *really* doing. Despite the success of the operation, she'd faced her own mortality and, having been in that situation myself, I knew what a big deal that was.

I drove up and spent the afternoon with her to keep her company and pamper her a bit, and just as I finished giving her a manicure she kept falling asleep in the chair. I could tell she was still pretty wiped out. But when I tried to sneak away to let her rest, she woke up. I seized the opportunity.

'Mum, I'm worried about you. Are you okay, you know . . . emotionally?'

I held my breath, hoping she'd open up to me, hoping she'd take the opportunity to lean on the person who'd leaned on her for so many years.

'Oh, I'm fine, Kate love. You don't need to worry about me; I should be worried about you, you're the one that's about to have a baby. What do you think of this colour on my fingers, does it suit me?'

I knew I couldn't drag it out of her: if she didn't want to talk to me about how she felt, I would have to respect that, but it's hard when someone you love is coping with something so big, feeling so seemingly alone, and yet still putting everyone else first.

Chapter Thirty-Five

'I'll go get the car warmed up!'

James called up the stairs to me. We had spent the week packing and repacking our hospital bags with nappies, wipes, several 'going-home' outfits for our daughter and PJs for me. We scrubbed the house from top to bottom, only stopping long enough to go out for a final meal at our favourite restaurant, just the two of us for the last time before we became three.

As I finished putting on my make-up for the evening, I sat and looked at myself briefly in the mirror, contemplating how different my life would be in just a matter of hours. I wondered how long it would be before I'd have this kind of time to get ready for a night out again. Would I be like my mum was when I was little? Sitting me on her hip and singing me songs?

James and I joked the whole drive to the restaurant about how it was the last time we'd leave the house without a mountain of bags and gear and buggies, and so promised one another we'd appreciate our final night of freedom without having to call on family to babysit.

After being shown to our table, I ordered a fruit juice and James a glass of champagne.

'James, can you believe what's going to happen to us tomorrow?'
I leaned back and rubbed my belly.

'She'll be here in the outside world – in twenty-four hours I'll be Mummy, you'll be Daddy.'

He was about to reply when the waiter bought two glasses of champagne to our table, with compliments from the owner. We knew him from eating there so often and sent our thanks. I agreed to drive us home and James drank both glasses over dinner. I could barely eat: a combination of being so pregnant there was no room for food and being so anxious about the following day. So, despite having wanted to make a night of it, we had decided by 9pm to go home and snuggle down while we waited for the next day to finally come around.

As we lay in bed that night, James held my tummy and we talked about how long ago the pregnancy test seemed. The trip to the supermarket to buy a better one, telling Mum and Dad, the first scan with Suzy, the time that had passed felt an eternity. Knowing we needed to get some serious rest, it was destined that neither of us would sleep a wink. We tossed and turned all night, each wrapped in our own thoughts and emotions. Sometime in the night, though, I miraculously drifted off. It felt like I'd only been asleep ten minutes when the alarm went off at 6am. It was time to get up and become parents. We got ready in near silence, feeling humbled by the significance of the day. As we closed the front door and got into the car, James voiced my thoughts out loud:

'Kate, the next time we open that door we'll be a family . . . the three of us. It has a nice ring to it, doesn't it?' I squeezed his hand and smiled as he started to drive.

We'd barely gone half a mile when I started crying. I felt completely overwhelmed with all kinds of emotions. My tummy was somersaulting with excitement, nerves, fear, bewilderment, anxiety and unbelievable happiness. The tears tumbled down my cheeks as I smiled and sniffed, half sobbing and half grinning at the thought of what was to come, and at how our whole world was about to change.

I had thought I'd be so matter-of-fact about it all until she actually arrived. I knew I'd fall apart when I eventually saw her, but I thought I'd hold it together before then. It's not like I was a stranger to hospitals. We checked in and were shown to a room where we'd wait until our scheduled surgery at 9am.

James settled into a seat and as I came out of the bathroom in the surgical gown and stockings, I started crying again. He gathered me up in a great big, safe hug and I tried to explain to him how I was feeling as I pressed my head into his chest.

'What if something goes wrong? What if something happens to our daughter? Usually I'm only responsible for me when I'm in hospital.'

I'd had surgical emphysema once before, following a throat operation when my oesophagus had been torn; air had escaped into my skin, which was painful and hard to recover from. I didn't care so much about myself, but I couldn't contemplate anything happening to my baby girl, who I'd been growing and taking care of inside my tummy all these months.

James said all the right things. 'Kate, keep calm, everything's going to be alright.'

But still, I prayed silently: 'Please, if something is going to go wrong, please let it happen to me and not to her. Please let her be okay.'

Even though I hadn't yet met our daughter, I already felt fiercely protective of her.

As the minutes ticked by, and with James's constant strength and reassurance, the fear at last turned into excitement. It was the first time ever, I felt happy to be in a surgical gown. I was called into the sterile operating theatre on the labour ward, which had been prepped for my C-section. They told James to wait outside, assuring him he could come in as soon as the spinal block to numb me had been administered.

The anaesthetist explained to me that in very rare cases paralysis is a side effect of the block. I knew he was just voicing the appropriate disclaimer so I could give informed consent, but it still felt scary. He rubbed some numbing lotion on the small of my back and I sat motionless, as he'd ordered me to, while he inserted the needle.

Meanwhile, the consultant talked me carefully through the procedure. The medical team helped me lie down because the anaesthetic had already taken effect and I couldn't move my legs. Then they started spraying freezing-cold liquid from my feet up, telling me to say when I could feel it. I gave a little shiver when I felt it near my chest and they nodded, confident that the block had worked and they could now prepare to deliver my baby. I started to tremble with nerves.

They called for James to come in. He stepped into the room, dressed in his surgical blues like a sexy Dr Doug from *ER*, and all my anxiety melted away. As we took a collective breath and prepared for our baby to be born, I thought about how I needed him beside me more than I needed anyone or anything in the world. How I depend on him, and how much happiness he brings me. I've let him in emotionally and shown him my vulnerabilities like I've never done with anyone outside my family, and I realised just how bonding this had been. With my hand in his, a feeling of relief flowed through me . . . ' James is here, I'll be okay.'

The doctor put up the screen so I couldn't see what was going on, and told me he was starting the op. They talked me through the whole thing, step by step, telling me when they were making the incision. I couldn't feel anything except a slight tugging; there was no pain at all.

James was giving me constant encouragement, telling me how well I was doing, but he stopped mid-sentence when we heard a strange little muffled sound. We stared at one another.

I blurted out, 'James, is that her? Is she here? Is she out?'

The doctor spoke before James had a chance.

'She's half in, half out, do you want to see her?'

We both nodded, wide-eyed and mute, and they pulled down the sheet. It was an absolute miracle – we could see our tiny daughter's face, her eyes closed tightly and a beautiful mop of dark hair on her head. All of a sudden she opened her arms towards me, spreading them like wings as wide as they would go, then she filled her lungs and started to cry as they finished pulling her out. I gasped, still gripping James's hand, my heart bursting with love and with tears of joy running down my face. I could only get three words out of my mouth, over and over and over again:

'That's our daughter! That's our daughter! That's our daughter! That's our daughter!!'

Chapter Thirty-Six

In the minutes that followed, as our daughter's life began, the flood of emotions that suddenly washed over me took me back to the thoughts I had when I was clinging on in intensive care immediately after the attack. People always say that your life flashes before your eyes before you die, and I remember thinking about being a child, about Mum, Dad, Paul and Suzy, about heaven, about religion. Today, lying there as my baby girl was swaddled, I realised her life was beginning in exactly the same place as where mine nearly ended; on an operating table in a hospital. I could smell the same antiseptic smells as I did back then, I could hear the same beeps of hospital machines, see doctors and nurses in their masks . . . the symmetry felt surreal, but also poignant and beautiful. I couldn't help but wonder whether this was always the greater plan, that these associations would come flooding back to me when I gave birth in order to replace the memories of what had happened to me. Maybe I didn't die that day because I was supposed to have a child, supposed to become a mum. I suddenly felt uplifted, like I'd fulfilled my destiny. I felt strong, proud and brave.

The doctor soon handed my daughter to me, but as I was still lying down and being sewn up they soon passed her to James, who cuddled her while they finished. As if she knew the weight of the moment too, we were all silent, lost in a moment of pure love. Neither James nor I could take our eyes off her, not even for a second. It seemed so other-worldly. We were overcome, and no words seemed big enough.

The nurses propped me up as soon as they could, and finally we had the moment we'd been longing for for the last nine months, being together as our own little family. James told his daughter how beautiful she was: our own perfect little person that together we'd created.

I was wheeled from the operating theatre to a recovery room on the next ward. James's mum and sister, Sue, had arrived during the operation, and Mum and Dad came bundling through the door the minute visiting hours started. They were both speechless, so I took the opportunity to introduce them.

'Mum, Dad, meet Belle . . .'

James and I had chosen her name a few weeks before she was born, but had kept it top secret. French for 'beautiful', it resonated massively with me; a tribute to those who helped me so much when I was treated in France, so the translation felt perfect. I'd also spent years trying to challenge people to see below the surface to the true beauty of a soul, a heart, a mind. Calling her Belle felt like a testament to my journey so far, and the one I'm still on.

Mum and Dad passed Belle between them, and showered her with kisses and cuddles, immediately embracing their new role as doting grandparents. They reminisced about when Paul, Suzy and I were each that small while Dad held and gazed at his granddaughter. Then Mum handed me a present. Unwrapping it gently, I smiled as I realised what it was. They'd given Belle a cuddly panda, almost identical to the ones we had been given as babies when we were each just hours old.

James's dad arrived soon after and we all talked about who she looked like and how beautiful she was. But while the grandparents cooed, I was starting to battle nausea – a combination of the anaesthetic and the painkillers I was on. James's dad had only been in the room a couple of minutes when I threw up in a cardboard bowl – pretty! Thankfully James was holding Belle at the time and as I struggled out of my gown and into a new one, I was glad Mum had reminded me to bring several pairs of PJs with me to hospital.

After visiting hours, everyone left James and me to spend some quiet time together and rest with the baby. Mum and Dad were staying at our house and although James wanted to spend the night sitting dutifully in the chair beside me and his newborn daughter, he eventually gave in to the call of a proper bed (and my gentle nagging to go get some sleep) and went home, promising he'd come straight back first thing in the morning.

For the first time since she'd been in my tummy, we were alone, my daughter and me. I sat gently talking to her, not sure of what to do.

'So, everyone's gone and it's just us now, Belle. What am I supposed to do? Fall asleep? I can't fall asleep when you're so new, I'll never fall asleep. I just want to keep looking at you. I'm your mum by the way.'

Despite the fact I knew I should try and rest, I ended up staring lovingly at Belle until the sun came up, drinking in every wrinkle, every line, imprinting the sight of her little rosebud lips on my heart and in my mind. I even pulled her cot into the bathroom with me while I went to the toilet – I didn't want her out of my sight for even a second.

I managed to persuade the doctor to discharge me after the afternoon rounds that second day, earlier than is recommended for a caesarean section, but I was desperate to leave so that I could show Belle to Mum and Dad again, and so that James, Belle and I could start being a family in our own home.

I was so nervous when James came to pick us up. Belle was all ready in a special going-home outfit: a beautiful pale-grey babygro that Mum had bought for her, and a little hat and mittens to shield her against the cool spring air.

James strapped her into the car seat while I lowered myself gently into the back seat beside her. I was taking painkillers but the incision point was still incredibly sore. I finally found a fairly comfy position and off we went. I've never known James drive so carefully in his life; we literally crawled most of the way home. Still, every single bump and pothole was agony. But I was far more worried about my daughter than myself. I kept glancing nervously from Belle to the other cars, wishing I'd printed a huge sign for the top of ours telling everyone to stay fifty metres back; that we had precious cargo on board.

As we pulled onto the driveway, I breathed a deep sigh of relief at having made it home in one piece. Mum and Dad formed the welcoming committee, taking the car seat from James as he helped me tiptoe the few steps into the house.

Putting Belle between us on the sofa as Mum made us tea, I was on a high. There weren't many words spoken by any of us (least of all Belle!). I watched her chest move up and down and couldn't believe my heart was capable of such depth, such capacity. I never knew I could love anyone so much.

None of us could take our eyes off her, our baby girl, a symbol of so much, of such a journey. She'd been growing for nine months but it felt like the last six years had all been working towards this moment – that this was the bright, shining light at the end of what had felt at times like a very long tunnel.

There are plenty of ways I know I'm a survivor. I'm reminded every day when I look in the mirror and it's rooted and intertwined with the creation of the Foundation. But becoming a mother, carrying my own baby and giving birth to my daughter will always be the most poignant and euphoric moment of my entire life. I took something back which my attackers had tried to take away from me and the victory felt exquisite.

All the survivors I speak to know the importance of fresh starts, new chapters and new beginnings. Moving forward will always keep the past behind you and starting a new role as a mother felt like the biggest step forward I'd made in all the years since the attack. With exhaustion and emotions flooding through me I sat in silence taking it all in and remembering every second.

Writing this now, even these words don't seem big enough for the feelings that coursed through me. There are simply no words big enough to describe how my heart felt as I watched my daughter sleep. My baby Belle. My Beautiful Ever After.

My darling Belle,

For so many years I forgot what it felt like to stroke a 'normal' cheek, to feel skin so soft it's barely there. You'll grow to learn that the skin on my face doesn't feel like yours. It's come from so many other places that it feels waxy, not soft and delicate like it should.

When you lie on my scarred chest to sleep, I see your perfect little head on one of the most damaged parts of me. It seems to be your favourite place to rest, as though you're telling me it doesn't matter, that even though it doesn't look like everyone else's, it has its own beauty for you.

Whenever you rest your hands on my disfigured, scarred body it feels like you're rubbing me better. Your touch gives me immeasurable strength, which I hope I can give back to you even in some small part. Your birth, your very existence, has changed my world, made me see things from a different perspective, made me cherish every step I've ever taken on my journey because each one was a step closer to you, to this.

And I'm not alone. Your birth has inspired thousands of people . . . I've had tweets, letters and emails from kind strangers all over the globe telling me that your arrival – and our journey together – has given them the hope and strength they needed to keep going when they felt like giving up, and to face the world feeling proud of who they are and to believe in a better future, no matter what.

My precious daughter, to me you are a living symbol of what it means to chase your dreams and never give up. Now it is your turn to find your way in this beautiful world, to spread your wings and soar in all your life's adventures. And I will be with you every step of the way.

Love,

Mummy xxx

Epilogue

As I write this, ten months on from the birth of our precious Belle, I now know for sure what before I only suspected. That my daughter wasn't just my Beautiful Ever After. She's my Beautiful New Beginning. Every day with her brings something new, something amazing, as she's learned to lift her head, roll, crawl, sit, eat solid food, and communicate in her own way; as she develops and grows. And as if Belle's arrival wasn't enough, in these ten short months there have been other – wonderful – new beginnings for me and my family. My brave mum has beaten cancer, and is ready to get started on the rest of her life. I'm so proud of her. And I know that one of the things she's looking forward to most is seeing me walk down the aisle. Because James and I will soon have our own new beginning, when we become husband and wife!

My family is fairly traditional, so back when I found out I was pregnant I was a bit scared to tell Mum and Dad. I felt like I was 16 and knocked up! I was worried they'd think, 'Well, you're not married, so this isn't really the right order.' And I couldn't help but feel a bit like that myself, too. When I was younger, I'd always imagined I'd meet a guy, move in with him, get engaged, get married and then have a baby, in that order. But with me and James, things just didn't happen that way. We both knew we wanted to be together forever, and we'd talked about marriage, but always in a casual sort of way, as something we knew we'd do one day but maybe not just yet. We also knew we both wanted kids, but because we didn't think I'd be able to conceive we hadn't expected it to happen any time soon, and we weren't being especially careful. When it did happen, we were overjoyed. But I also had this nagging feeling that I wished things were happening in the right order. That in turn made me feel ungrateful and selfish, as I remembered times in my life when I'd been desperately lonely and feared I'd never even have a boyfriend, let alone a child, yet here I was now, thinking: 'If only I was married!' So I tried to take a step back. 'Hang on a minute, Katie,' I told myself. 'Look how your whole life has happened! Did you ever seriously think any of these events would happen and that you'd be standing here today in the position you are now?' Once I managed to get a bit of perspective, I stopped worrying about what the 'right order' was and just tried to enjoy my pregnancy.

Even so, each time there was a special occasion, I couldn't help wondering if maybe James would pop the question. I'd build it up in my mind, thinking, it's bound to be today! My thirtieth birthday is a good example. I thought, not only is it a landmark birthday but I'm also pregnant with our child, so I was convinced this was it. I even went as far as texting my friends, saying, 'I think he's going to ask!'

On the morning of my birthday, James brought me breakfast in bed. Right, I thought, here we go! On the tray was a big box. 'Aha!' I smiled to myself. 'I know his game – he's put the ring in a big box to trick me.' I opened it, getting ready to act all surprised, and there it was – a Michael Kors watch. Which was absolutely gorgeous of course, and normally I'd have been so ecstatic with a present like that, but it just wasn't quite what I was expecting. Luckily I managed to hide my disappointment.

It went on like this for a while, with me secretly feeling a little bit disappointed each time a significant event came to an end and he still hadn't asked me. A trip to Paris. Our anniversary. I realised I was spoiling every big occasion by building it up and then coming away feeling disappointed. I told myself it had to stop, and tried to put it out of mind. And I did manage to forget about it because suddenly we had so much else going on in our lives. As we got nearer to my due date, there was loads to do in preparation for Belle's arrival. Then she was born, and our days (and nights!) became pretty much non-stop. By the time we'd got used to having Belle in our lives, it was time for me to go back to work and things got even busier. So that's how it had all been left, and when the night of the proposal did finally arrive I had absolutely no idea at all.

It was December and I'd been filming *Bodyshockers* five or six days a week since August. Things had been so busy for months that James and I had barely had any quality time together for ages, so we agreed we needed a date night. We chose a rare evening when we were both free and made a plan. We decided it would be nicer to stay in – we'd both been working so hard that we'd hardly been at home, and we just wanted to enjoy being in our own house together and spend some time with Belle instead of leaving her with a babysitter. To make it a bit special, we decided to cook a three-course dinner, using fancy recipes we'd chosen from cookbooks, and score ourselves points like on *Come Dine With Me*. We decided to get champagne, and set the table really nicely, make it feel a bit like a restaurant.

So this was all planned, the date was set, and we were both really looking forward to it. However, a couple of days beforehand, I had a call from my agent saying I was needed in Dundee for filming as Channel 4 had found this guy who was covered head to toe in tattoos, perfect for the show. And unfortunately it was going to clash with our date night. When I'm in filming mode I have to be really flexible and go wherever I'm needed at short notice. And because *Bodyshockers* was due to broadcast at the start of January, it was on a very tight deadline. I had no choice but to cancel our dinner. I messaged James to reschedule, not expecting it to be a problem because normally he's very understanding about anything to do with my career, always supporting me, never questioning or holding me back. But on this occasion he reacted really strangely, responding with, 'No, you can't!' 'I have to!' I told him. 'You know I'm in the middle of this project, that has to be my priority.' That's just how it is with my work, and he's totally familiar with that. But he was really upset and begged me to cancel. At that point I did start to wonder what the big deal was. I had been looking forward to our date, too, but I could hardly tell work I was cancelling filming so that I could stay at home with my boyfriend to have dinner and then probably an early night! So off I went to Dundee and in the end James calmed down and we managed to reschedule our dinner for the Sunday.

As it happened, on the Sunday I was asked to do a last-minute press shoot for *Bodyshockers*, to get pictures with some of the most extreme contributors – people with facial tattoos, for example, or who were addicted to plastic surgery – which would be syndicated out to all the magazines. I asked James if he wanted to come along to the shoot to meet the photographer, Ray, who's a good friend of mine. He's photographed me for years, right from when

I was single, fresh after the attack, all the way through to now. James agreed to come, and because the shoot was up in town, we thought it would be a nice treat for Belle if afterwards we popped into Winter Wonderland in Hyde Park. I wondered if trying to do our fancy dinner that night was all a bit too much. When you have a small baby, attempting to squeeze more than two things into a day usually ends in disaster. Plus it was Sunday night, so we both had work the next morning. But when I said all this to James, he got quite flustered and annoyed with me. He was determined we should go ahead with our plan. I couldn't work out why he was so adamant about doing it that night and thought he was being a bit stupid, but since it was my fault we'd had to postpone I just bit my tongue and went along with it.

At the shoot that day, Ray offered to take some off-the-record photos of the three of us – me, James and Belle – for us to put up around our house. He's such a lovely guy. So it means I've got gorgeous family photos from the day we got engaged, although obviously I didn't realise the significance until later. James had never done a photo shoot in his life so I thought he'd enjoy it. I'd also been conscious that he might have felt left out when I did my *Hello!* photo shoot with Belle after her birth, so this seemed a nice way to make it up to him. I laughed so much when he asked, 'Will I wear makeup!?' 'If you want to!!!' I sniggered. So he did! My hair and makeup people sat him down and put some makeup on his face, and afterwards he kept it on! On our way to Winter Wonderland I swear he kept glancing at himself in shop and car windows. And when he said, 'I really like this – do you think I should get it for when I go clubbing,' that was it – I just couldn't control myself any longer! In hysterics, I told him: 'You're a dad! You don't *go* clubbing! Calm yourself down!'

We got to Winter Wonderland and looked around for a bit, but it wasn't long before Belle started to get tired. Knowing we still had our whole evening to sort out, we decided to call it a day and go home. We rushed back and got ourselves dressed up. I chose a black dress, put my hair in rollers and re-did my makeup. At the time, I had an eye infection, so one of my eyes was taped shut with surgical tape. (Looking back, I can't believe he chose that day of all days to propose to me! Not exactly the glamorous look I'd have picked for the moment I got asked to be someone's wife!) Anyway, once I'd put eye-makeup on just one side and added a single false lash, I said I'd get our first course sorted while James fed Belle, and then we'd swap over so I could put her down to bed. I went downstairs and saw that James had set up the dining table with a tablecloth, champagne bucket and candles. It looked lovely, but I thought nothing of it because we'd often had evenings like this before.

Once Belle was settled in her cot, we sat down to our starter: homemade canapés of mini toad-in-the-hole, drizzled with honey and with a creamy dip on the side. James had made us each a delicious minty vodka cocktail to drink before we cracked open the champagne. Right from the start, he was behaving weird. I leant over to get something and accidentally knocked a bottle of balsamic vinegar. Even though it didn't spill, he was really startled! I picked it back up, thinking he must be tired and overwhelmed from our long day. 'Sorry,' he said, 'I'm really nervous.' At that, I burst out laughing! Why would he be nervous!? We were sitting in our own house with our baby upstairs, and me with my taped-up eye – what, was he worried I might never ring him again or something!? I thought, 'God! We're well past that, how silly!' I still didn't put two and two together!

We moved on to our main course, which James had cooked

– fish with capers, spinach and a mango sauce. James started to relax and everything seemed more normal as we chatted and ate. He cleared the plates and then asked me to check on the dessert (chocolate mousse, which we'd made earlier and put in the fridge to set) while he went upstairs to the loo. I raised my eyebrows – he was being weird again. We have a downstairs toilet, so why was he off upstairs? In fact, there was only one possible explanation and I didn't want *that* image in my head during a romantic dinner. 'Charming,' I thought! 'I guess romance truly is dead!'

James was gone for a while so I took the opportunity to check Twitter and Instagram, share a snap of our date night and reapply my lipstick. When he finally arrived back at the table I saw he'd put a folded newspaper on my placemat. 'How rude,' I thought! Why was he reading the paper at the table when we were supposed to be having quality time together? 'Put that away,' I told him. 'No,' he said, 'You need to take a look because it just came through the door with a note saying "Read page 4".' At this, I panicked. It was 10pm on a Sunday night. Who the hell had approached our house at this time – and why? How had they got past our intercom entry system to reach our letterbox? I felt really quite scared. 'Don't touch it,' I snapped. 'It could be a trap!' And I set off upstairs to check the CCTV.

But James was calling me back saying 'No, no, no!' and telling me to calm down. 'Will you please just read page 4!' he insisted. Reluctantly I came back to the table, thinking, oh god no, what's happened? What has someone put in the paper about us? We try to keep a low profile, and we especially don't want Belle being photographed. So I was afraid someone had written something horrible about me or – worse – about James or Belle, and he didn't know how to tell me. I'd tried so hard to protect them both from anything bad happening but maybe I'd missed something.

I sat down and opened the paper, dreading what I was about to see.

I turned to page 4 and there was a huge headline that said: 'Exclusive News: Katie Will You Marry Me?' and a subheading underneath, that read: 'What Will Katie Say? James Waits Nervously for the Answer!'

I still didn't get it. I thought it must be an article about Katie Price, or maybe Katie Hopkins. I couldn't work out why he was showing me this. I just wanted to eat our chocolate mousse and get on with our evening; it wasn't the time to be reading some gossip page! But James still seemed to be waiting for my reaction, so I scanned down the article. It was all about how he'd felt when he'd met me, what we'd brought to each other's lives. It talked about how he felt I'd bettered him as a person, and the positive changes he'd seen in me that he hoped were because of him. It said how we should always stay together because we enrich each other's lives. It was really deep stuff for a builder! Still struggling to understand, my next theory was that maybe he was pitching for a column. I wondered if this was some kind of draft that he wanted my feedback on. I read further, feeling more and more confused. The article went on to talk about the reasons he'd held back from asking me to marry him, but why now was the right time, and how having a daughter together had really sealed things for him. It finished with 'Will you marry me?'

By now, I'd realised it wasn't a column. Then I thought, 'Oh my god, he'd better not have put this in the paper.' Even if he was trying for a big romantic gesture, this was the sort of thing that really should be kept private. James was sitting to the side of my taped-up eye so all the time I was reading I couldn't see him properly. I turned to look at him and was baffled to see that rather than sitting in his seat he seemed to be lying on the floor. It was all so surreal!

Of course, he wasn't really lying on the floor – he was actually down on one knee! I heard the words 'So will you marry me?' and he held out a Haribo ring. I was so taken aback, still trying to work out why it was in the paper and how everything connected up, but somehow I managed to get some words out: 'Uh, yeah … okay, yes I will, yeah!' I'd finally worked out what had just happened, and suddenly I couldn't remember how to talk! James put the Haribo ring on my finger and it all just hit me.

Strangely enough, that moment when I realised what he'd just asked was comparable to some of my very worst moments. It's a surreal feeling when you think something – whether good or bad – could never, *ever* happen, but then it does. It totally takes you off course. I'm sure most girls have planned what they'd wear, what they'd say, and how it would all go – but all of that went out of the window. I was at my most unglamorous, at the end of a long, tiring day, with my eye all puffy and taped up. The conversation wasn't full of nice lines, I just sort of stuttered and gabbled away in surprise! But I wouldn't have changed it. And in the end I'm so glad it was a surprise and I didn't force or guilt-trip him into it by piling on the pressure; that he asked me when he wanted to, not because I expected him to do it on a certain occasion.

Once I'd got over the initial shock, we sat back down and immediately rang my parents. Mum and Dad both started crying! They were so happy for us. My dad had actually known this was coming because James had asked him permission at my charity ball a month before. At the ball James had told my dad how proud he was seeing me up on the stage and that he just knew there and then that he wanted to marry me. My dad had cried that night, too, but I'd thought it was because he was drunk! He'd managed to keep it a complete secret from my mum, which must have been tough because they're so close, but I guess he wanted her to hear it from me. In the past, I know my parents were scared I'd never have this. They once thought I'd be living at home forever, on disability benefit, and that my mum would have to give up work to look after me. That's the prospect the doctors and psychologists gave them. So every step of my career has amazed and astounded them – not because they didn't think I was capable – but because it seemed impossible to come back from something so awful, especially with the permanent shadow of knowing that one day my attackers will come out of prison. And even when I'd made more progress than anyone ever expected – moved back to London, started working for Channel 4, running the Foundation and writing books – they still knew the real me and that underneath I was desperate for a normal girl's life with the companionship of a boyfriend. They wanted it for me but knew they couldn't promise it. They realised it was a tough world out there. So, for them, everything that goes right in my life now must seem like an amazing bonus.

I guess my engagement is like a giant thank you to my family for all their support. I feel guilty for what they went through as a result of my attack. For years I felt like a burden to them, so now it's like I'm giving back. That made it especially hard when I found out Mum had cancer. I just prayed: 'Please let her live to experience all the things that a mum *should* have from a daughter, because she's only experienced all the things a mum should never even know *exists* for their daughter. Please let me be able to support her through this, please let her survive to see her granddaughter.' My prayers were answered. I'm so glad she was able to be part of everything that happened last year, with my pregnancy and Belle, and it's a dream come true that she'll be at my wedding. It's just so amazing to share it all with her.

Next we rang James's parents and his sister, who were over the moon as well. Afterwards they sent me the loveliest messages, telling me how glad they were to have me in their family, as their daughter-in-law. I hadn't realised they felt that way. I remember in the past once fearing I'd never get a boyfriend because other people's parents would think, 'Why can't he go out with someone normal?' When I first fell in love with James, I was reluctant to meet his family because I didn't want it to ruin everything. Before meeting them, I was so nervous. 'Please don't let them take him away from me,' I prayed. But it was completely fine and they were totally welcoming. In reality, it was never an issue at all, it was all in my head. And here I was today, receiving the most beautiful messages from them. Their reaction to our engagement was the total opposite of everything I'd once feared to be true.

After we put the phone down, there was this really weird anti-climax. What were we supposed to do now? We felt like we wanted to go and buy a megaphone and shout out to everyone that we were getting married! Instead we sat down and ate the chocolate mousse (which wasn't even very nice!), drank another glass of champagne, and just sort of paced the house! I looked at the clock and it was gone 11pm. Belle had a swimming lesson in the morning, so we needed to be up early. Oh well, time for bed. What a strange end to the evening. I checked on Belle – fast asleep throughout the whole thing! – and got into bed. Of course, I could barely sleep. I lay there thinking about how I'd left my house that morning as one person and now I was another person; how one chapter had ended and another one had begun …

It's funny how, even though James and I were already com-mitted in many ways – living together, with a baby and a mortgage, suddenly those words had made everything feel different. More secure somehow. I'm excited that we'll soon all have the same surname, be a proper family unit. Being able to say 'I'm someone's fiancée' feels amazing, and I'm looking forward to calling myself a 'wife'. When I took Belle to mum-and-baby groups, other women would talk about their husbands and I'd feel silly that I couldn't use that word. I thought – oh, I'm not a wife. I'm just a girlfriend. It sounded childish and temporary. So I did struggle with that label a bit, even though I've learned the hard way that labels don't always mean much – you could be a 'wife' to a terrible man who cheats on you and treats you badly, yet I was a 'girlfriend' to someone who treats me amazingly. I know that's what should matter, not the title given to it. But having spent years feeling like I could never have this, could never play this role in society, I can't help but be excited. I can't stop looking at my engagement ring. James and I designed it together, not long after he proposed, so it's really personal and exactly what I wanted. (I put the Haribo ring in the freezer so hopefully it will also last forever).

One of the first people I wanted to tell, after our families, was Mr Jawad, my surgeon. He's in Pakistan at the moment, setting up a new burns clinic, so I emailed him to share the news and invite him to our wedding. He sent me the most amazing reply telling me how happy he is for me and my family, and that it was the most wonderful thing he'd heard in 2014. He thanked me for always remembering him and told me how honoured he'd be to come. He said he'd always been confident this day would arrive and that I remain a constant source of pride for him. I used to think about my wedding (as any girl does, even before they've met a guy!) and knew that if it ever did happen, I'd want Mr Jawad there. I see him as a bit of a father figure and will definitely be planning the wedding around his availability.

It's easy to forget that these consultants are parents themselves

– he has a daughter the same age as me. Now that I understand the demands of being a parent, I'm even more grateful for everything he did for me. What if he'd been too busy to take me on as a patient? Where would I be now? I look after my own charity and also support two other charities each year, but I constantly get emails asking me to help with other causes and fundraising. Now that I've got Belle, it's harder than ever to find time. I've had moments when I've looked at my diary and realised I can only do something if I use the time I've put aside for her. Then I put myself in other people's shoes and think: what if I'd reached out for help and somebody had turned me down? I'd have been heartbroken. If Mr Jawad hadn't accepted me as a patient, I probably wouldn't be getting married, I probably wouldn't have Belle, I certainly wouldn't be who I am today. And I wonder, can I be like Mr Jawad to someone else? If I say no, am I taking that away from someone? That's one of my big worries. So I always try and do everything I can, but the sad reality is I can't help everyone.

Being a parent brings its own forms of guilt, too. When I'm helping other women through the charity, or interviewing them for my TV series, people often tell me my daughter is so lucky to have a mum like me. And I'm flattered, but can't help but feel bad that in reality Belle rarely gets a piece of me. Thanks to work, I'm so often not with her. I know it's something a lot of working mums struggle with. Luckily, with my job, once Belle's walking and talking she'll be able to come along and volunteer, and be a part of it. I hope she'll learn that it's part of our responsibility as women and good people to make up for the terrible things that happen to others for no good reason.

Because so many people have touched my life and helped me, now I feel it's my duty to give something back, like a domino effect. It's my turn in the Mexican wave. Poor James has to be the backbone of the entire operation, holding everything together behind the scenes! If my filming or work runs later than expected, James will feed Belle, bath her, put her to bed, and then sort the house and our dinner. If I have to go away for filming, he usually stays at home and holds the fort. Many guys just wouldn't do that. I guess I'm not an easy person to live with, but he doesn't seem to mind. He's a strong, easy-going person, with his own career, and no desire for fame or admiration from strangers. He's just so satisfied with his life and that's what makes him so supportive.

We haven't picked a date for the wedding yet. James proposed just before Christmas, so things were pretty busy, then we went straight into the launch of *Bodyshockers*, and after that we went on holiday. So we've not had a chance to make plans, but I wouldn't mind getting married this year because I'd rather not have a long engagement. I just want to make it official! September's a possibility, although we've already got three weddings in the family this year, and my brother has to come all the way from America, so it might not work. Next January is another option. In terms of what kind of wedding we'd like, for the ceremony I want to stay fairly traditional – I believe in God so I'd like religious vows and a vicar to marry us. When I was initially recovering from my burns, one of the first public places I was brave enough to go to was our local church. It felt like a safe haven. The vicar there mentored me through some very hard times. I don't know if he realises how key he was to my early recovery, but I'd love to track him down and ask him to marry us. He gave me hope when I felt hopeless.

In other ways I'll probably break tradition – for example, I really want to give a speech myself. I have so many people to thank that I don't just want to sit there mute! And I would like my surgeon

Mr Jawad to be at the top table, even though it's normally reserved for the parents and best man. He's just so important to me.

For the reception, we're torn. It would be amazing to throw a massive party and invite everyone who's ever supported me, including fellow burns survivors who I've known right from the start of my recovery. We've also thought about doing something more intimate. We're not sure yet, but what we do know is that since everything's pretty unconventional in our lives and our relationship, we're just going to have the wedding we *want* rather than what people expect us to do. Maybe we'll go completely alternative! I'm a massive Michael Jackson fan … perhaps we'll have a Michael Jackson themed wedding! We could use an old disused theatre as the venue, and do it all up like one of his music videos. Who knows?! We figure we might as well make it the best and craziest party of our lives. Having said that, don't expect anything *too* way out. We won't be arriving in a pumpkin!

As for my wedding dress, I've already had some wonderful offers from people to design me something. I'm not really a designer girl – I usually wear high-street clothes – so I'd just like something simple, probably quite loose-fitting and flowy, what you'd imagine for a barefoot beach wedding, though maybe with a bit of vintage lace. Definitely no corsets or boning, and no big net underskirts. I'll probably wear my hair down with a very simple veil. And I know the colour scheme I want for the bridesmaids and all the flowers. I'd really like it to be yellow. Not only will yellow look lovely with Belle's skin tone, but it's such a happy, positive colour, full of sunshine and happiness.

When I stop to think, I do feel quite nervous about the wedding, because I can't help but remember it's is the one day when all eyes are on you, and sometimes that's not a great feeling.

It's quite nerve-wracking to be centre of attention for a whole day – especially as I've spent parts of my life trying to avoid anyone looking at me. At my charity ball I always feel more nervous than when I do any public speaking or filming, because everyone in the room is someone I deeply care about, who has supported me along the way: family, doctors, colleagues, the corporates who fund the charity. They are all real people to me and it really matters to me what they think. I imagine a wedding will feel similar, which does make me nervous. But in a good way.

The public response to our engagement has been overwhelming. Even in comparison with when I announced being pregnant. It's made my phone crash so many times. There are two types of messages: some people get in touch to say they are genuinely happy for us, as they would be for friends – so lovely and sincere. And others contact me to say it's given them hope when they're really struggling. I'm pleased when I hear this, because I remember thinking there was nobody out there like me, nobody who had a happy ending I could hope for. We've also received lots of cards and presents from people we don't know – I've made a big memory box and kept them all.

It's like things have come full circle. Once, people I'd never met were horrified and sad and heartbroken for me when they heard the news story about the attack; now people I don't know are ecstatic and happy for me. It's an amazing thing. I've seen two extremes and witnessed how people react to both. It's like having a massive extended family, which is such a warm feeling to have in your life. I definitely believe in good energy so it can only be a good thing having so many people wanting the best for you. I'm so grateful to everyone for their support and will be thinking of them all fondly as I make my way down the aisle, whenever that might be!

Acknowledgments

So many people have made it possible for me to continue to tell my story. I would like to thank all the people I have never met who continue to support me, encourage me and allow me to grow. It's been brilliant to be able to talk some of you on Twitter. I am who I am because of the acceptance and love the general public has shown towards me, and I'm truly grateful for it.

To my Family: Mum, Dad, Paul and Suzy. If we had known six years ago that I would be writing a book entitled *Beautiful Ever After*, I don't think we would have quite believed it, but I got here with my happy ending and it's due to you and the unconditional love and support you have always shown me, so thank you.

Thank you to all the team in the Katie Piper Foundation office and our board of trustees. Your passion, dedication and caring attitude are inspiring. I feel so very proud and lucky to have people like you around me – you have taken the Foundation to new heights and in turn have helped so many other 'Katies'. From me, and from all the other burns survivors, thank you. To the friends, beneficiaries and fundraisers of KPF, thank you for sharing your stories and your courage and also for giving up your precious time to help us realize our vision.

Thank you to the incredible team at Quercus for believing in me, encouraging me creatively and enabling me to able to share my experiences with others: Jenny Heller, Ione Walder, Bethan Ferguson, Hannah Robinson, Richard Milner, David North, Caroline Butler, Dave Murphy and Clare O'Reilly. You have helped me translate the thoughts and experiences from my head into this book, and it has been a really great honour to have had the privilege of working with you all again. A huge thank you for all of the time, knowledge and expertise each of you has given.

Thank you also to my agent and the team at Fresh Partners for all your professional support, advice and baby tips! Thank you also to all at Plank PR for your support and knowledge.

My last thank you goes to James and Belle; without you this book would have told a very different story. Both of you are the lights in my life that will never go out. James, you are a beautiful person who has taught me so much about myself and about the world. Thank you for your love and support in everything that I do. Belle Elizabeth, my precious gift, thank you for completing me. My new family – I love you.